LINKS ALONG THE LINE

The Story of the Development of Golf
Between Liverpool and Southport

Lancashire & Yorkshire Railway – Where to Golf.

LINKS ALONG THE LINE

The Story of the Development of Golf Between Liverpool and Southport

Harry Foster

"The motor car has made golf in many ways easier and pleasanter, but has it not in some small degree impaired the old comradeship of the game? Once upon a time there was an obvious morning train to the course; everybody used it and matches were made up on the journey . . . In the result, I fancy, people played with a greater variety of partners than they do today."

Bernard Darwin *The Pleasures of Golf*

First published in the U.K. in 1996 by
The Birkdale and Ainsdale Historical Research Society,
20, Blundell Drive, Birkdale, Southport, PR8 4RG

ISBN 0-9510905-2-6

Produced for the Society by
Sutton Publishing Ltd, Stroud, Glos.
Printed in Great Britain

CONTENTS

BIRKDALE AND AINSDALE HISTORICAL RESEARCH SOCIETY

Links along the Line is the sixth in the Society's series of publications and shares the aims of its predecessors. We are attempting to find new material about the district and then to present it in a manner which will bring pleasure and enjoyment to readers. We are always grateful to have access to any historical material, particularly old photographs, which relates to Birkdale and Ainsdale.

Sylvia Harrop,
Publications Editor.

PREVIOUS PUBLICATIONS

Sylvia Harrop, *Old Birkdale and Ainsdale: Life on the south-west Lancashire Coast 1600–1851*, B & A Historical Research Society (1985).

Peggy Ormrod, *Birkdale and Ainsdale Past and Present: The 1845 tithe map superimposed on a modern street plan*, B & A Historical Research Society (1987).

Sylvia Harrop (ed.), *Families and Cottages of Old Birkdale and Ainsdale*, Carnegie Publishing (1992).

Harry Foster, *New Birkdale: The Growth of a Lancashire Seaside Suburb 1850–1912*, Alan Sutton Publishing (1995).

Harry Foster, *Southport: A Pictorial History*, Phillimore (1995).

Further details from: Mrs P.M.Perrins,
Secretary, Birkdale and Ainsdale Historical Research Society,
20 Blundell Drive,
Birkdale,
Southport,
PR8 4RG.

ILLUSTRATIONS

PREFACE

DR. DAVID MARSH

Harry Foster was a boyhood rugby hero of mine at school, with Waterloo and for Lancashire. Little did I know that later in our lives we should be playing together in the same rugger team and that on one Saturday evening, in order to prevent a long wait in the casualty department, I would employ my surgical skills to repair a gash over his eye with a darning needle borrowed from a lady supporter of the club we had just played. A good result – we trained later that week – and a lasting friendship.

Now I am admiring his history of golf on the south-west Lancashire coast – *Links Along the Line* – which helps us to understand how on this stretch of sand dunes such a wonderful collection of golf links exists. These are world-famous courses upon which great deeds have been performed by famous players – some of them local.

Around the turn of the century the skilled and the good players were often members of a number of these clubs and evidence in the club histories shows such players winning the important medals of many clubs. Nevertheless, the inter-club fellowship is still very evident, long-standing matches are continued and social occasions shared.

Perhaps the only certain descendants from the days of the golfing pioneers on these links are the furry rabbits which burrow in the dunes. Having survived the local hazards and scourge of disease, they continue to be a nightmare to all keepers of greens.

It is with much pleasure that I write and wish success to this book, which will surely become an important addition to a local golfer's library.

ACKNOWLEDGEMENTS

One of the themes of this book is the notion of a community of golfers in the clubs along the south-west Lancashire coast. In preparing this book I am grateful for the assistance and co-operation that I have received from within the Royal Liverpool, West Lancashire, Formby, Hesketh, Royal Birkdale, Southport and Ainsdale and Hillside golf clubs. This book has a rationale of its own and is not a synopsis of the excellent existing club histories, nevertheless it owes a debt to the work of those who compiled these histories – John Beherend, Guy Farrar, Leslie Edwards, Fred Lowe, Ivor Thomas, Keith Hick, George Mitchell, Tony Johnson, Philip Irlam, Mrs Audrey Pratt, Mrs C.J. Dickinson, Mrs Nancy Dixon and John Spence. Special thanks go to Dr. David Marsh for writing the preface for this book. As a former Captain of both the Walker Cup team and the Royal and Ancient Golf Club of St Andrews, David is one of our most distinguished amateur golf players and administrators.

For the provision of illustrations I would like to thank: the golf clubs listed above; Mr Tony Wray, Keeper of Art Galleries and Museums for Sefton M.B., Miss Margaret Proctor, formerly Archivist for the Merseyside Record Office, Messrs Keith Bond, Terence Burgess, Mark Chatterton, John Donoghue, Chris Foster, Peter Gibb, Bryan Kernaghan, Alan Marshall, David Regan, Ian Simpson, Alan R. Whittaker and Geoff Wright.

Finally thanks are due to the members of the Birkdale and Ainsdale Historical Research Society, particularly Sylvia Harrop, the Society's Publications Editor, and Pat Perrins the Society's Secretary; Alan R. Whittaker for the photographic work, David Foster for the graphics, Chris Driver for computer assistance, and to my wife Thelma, who after tolerating my absence on the golf course and at Club functions on so many occasions was still prepared to read the text.

Harry Foster

CHAPTER ONE

INTRODUCTION

"Almost with one consent, the landowners of the Liverpool district have united in offering facilities for golf, rightly recognising a golf club as a nucleus of a residential estate. The railway companies are following suit. Golfers pay ground rents in one case, and take contract tickets in the other. As the houses multiply, there is no end to the revenue of the ground landlord or of the railway company. Small wonder, then, that both these monopolists recognise in golf a sort of benificent farming who use the deserts of sand."

Southport Visiter March 1904.

Golf has been played in Scotland for hundreds of years. There it was the people's game, enjoyed by all sections of society. It was played on available open spaces, without formal rules, fairways or greens. Golfers would choose the land they thought suitable, usually pasture cropped short by sheep, and cut a hole with a long bladed knife. At the seaside, where the game was played on the agriculturally impoverished sandy strips which formed the 'link' between land and sea, the holes were frequently marked with seagull feathers. It was not until 1754 that the members of the Society of St Andrews' Golfers established a set of thirteen rules, and it was the Old Course at St Andrews which set the pattern of eighteen separate holes. Formal teeing grounds were still unknown. Players had to tee off at a point a certain number of golf club lengths from the last hole played.

It is said that when James VI of Scotland came south to succeed Elizabeth his adherents brought to the court, at Greenwich, their native passion for the 'Royal and Ancient Game' and started to play at nearby Blackheath. Nevertheless, despite this aristocratic introduction of the game to England, it was nearly 200 years before the Royal Blackheath Golf Club was founded in

1787. Again it was immigrant Scots who were responsible. By 1818 a similar group had started to play in Lancashire at Kersal Moor, Manchester. There is evidence to demonstrate that by the mid-nineteenth century there was a growing number of expatriate Scots playing the game, albeit informally. These economic migrants, attracted south by the commercial opportunities afforded by the Industrial Revolution, figured prominently amongst the founders who formalised golf in England into the format of clubs. That is where groups of golfers played matches and competitions on a course, with a clubhouse, that they maintained at their corporate expense. The earlier expansion of public school education, with its emphasis on team games, had produced men who were ripe for conversion to the 'Royal and Ancient Game.' Although golfing novices, these men of wealth and position, with ample time for leisure, enthusiastically joined the experienced Scottish players in founding clubs. In doing so they put their own mark on the game in England, making it a socially elitist sport.

The 'Royal and Ancient Game' was brought to the north-west coast by a group of Liverpool gentlemen with strong Scottish connections. They included James Muir Dowie of West Kirby, whose contribution is marked by a hole bearing his name on the Royal Liverpool course, and his father-in-law Robert Chambers. The latter was a resident of Edinburgh, and one of Scotland's leading amateur golf players. Seeking an opportunity to play golf, the group sought permission to play on 'The Warren' adjoining the Royal Hotel at Hoylake. Part of this area was used as a racecourse by the Liverpool Hunt Club, and, having been cropped by sheep and rabbits, the golfers judged the terrain to be suitable for their purpose. From such informal beginnings the Liverpool Golf Club was founded in 1869. The club initially used rooms at the Royal Hotel. John Ball sen., the landlord became a stalwart of the Club, whilst his son John was to become one of the all-time great golfers, winning the Amateur Championship eight times and the Open once. The original nine-hole course was laid out by George Morris, who was Robert Chambers' personal professional. George's son, Jack Morris, was appointed professional to care for the course, to make clubs and to give lessons. The men of the Liverpool business community were quick to support the new Club, which soon had over 100 members. From as early as 1870, the active support of the wealthy members enabled the Club to sponsor competitions for the leading professionals of the day. An article in *The Field* noted that:

> "The Club which is very prosperous offers great inducements to visit their links and the liberality of individual members is unbounded. No example is spared in bringing the best professionals from distant links and everything is done to encourage the Royal and Ancient game. Young golfers on the Hoylake links have but more opportunity of learning the style and stance than beginners on any other English links."[1]

HOYLAKE RACES,

TUESDAY AND WEDNESDAY,

AUGUST 4TH AND 5TH, 1846.

FIRST DAY.

The Hooton Park Stakes, of 3 sovereigns each, with £15 added; for *bona fide* Hunters—Heats, twice round

Mr Tempest b g T'auld Squire, 5 yrs... yellow and black cap
Mr. Grace's ns. b h Dragsman, aged .. blue and black cap
Mr. Shephard's b g Mudlark, aged .... red and blue cap

The Selling Stakes of 2 sovs. each, with £10 added by the fund—Heats, twice round

Mr. Graham's ch m Sunbeam, aged.. blue and yellow cap
Mr. Tempest b f by St. Martin, 3 yrs .. yellow and black cap
Mr. Davie's b f Bay Fanny, 3 yrs .... scarlet and black cap

The Adelphi Cup, value £10, clear, the gift of Mr. Cleave, Adelphi Hotel, Woodside.

Dr. Furgison's ch h Pill Box, 5 yrs .. crimson and yellow cap
Mr. Tempest b g T'auld Squire, 5 yrs.. yellow and black cap
Mr. Parson's b g Greenfinch, aged .. scarlet and black cap

J. GRIFFITH, PRINTER, BIRKENHEAD.

1. Hoylake Races' Card, 1846. Hoylake's racing heritage is remembered in the names of two of the Royal Liverpool Club's holes – Course and Stand – whilst the saddling bell still hangs in the clubhouse.

3

Golf was firmly established in the north-west and its foundations at Hoylake were secure. The course was extended to eighteen holes in 1871, the year in which the Club received its Royal designation, as a result of the patronage of His Royal Highness The Duke of Connaught. A new railway line gave access to the Club to members of Liverpool's merchant class. Despite having to cross the river for business, increasing numbers chose to settle south of the Mersey.

Many of Britain's great golf courses are associated with railway lines. Indeed, across the Mersey from the Royal Liverpool Club, on the south-west Lancashire coast a small length of the commuter line – Merseyrail's Northern Line between Liverpool and Southport – runs through possibly the greatest concentration of championship golf courses in the country. It is these courses that form the subject of this book – *Links along the Line*. The neighbouring links of the West Lancashire, Formby, Southport and Ainsdale, and Hillside golf clubs all have holes where a slice or hook can put the ball over the railway fence and 'out of bounds'. Although the Royal Birkdale links do not adjoin this

2. Hoylake – Punchbowl Hole. The fourball in this watercolour painting by J. Michael Brown includes the Royal Liverpool Club's two great champions – John Ball and Harold Hilton.

4

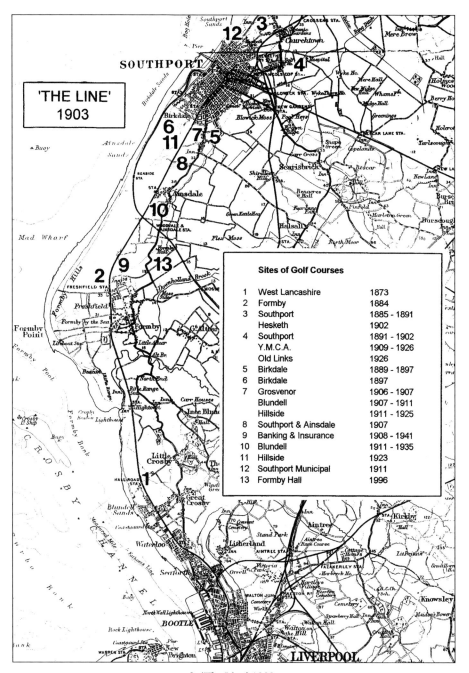

'THE LINE'
1903

Sites of Golf Courses

1	West Lancashire	1873
2	Formby	1884
3	Southport	1885 - 1891
	Hesketh	1902
4	Southport	1891 - 1902
	Y.M.C.A.	1909 - 1926
	Old Links	1926
5	Birkdale	1889 - 1897
6	Birkdale	1897
7	Grosvenor	1906 - 1907
	Blundell	1907 - 1911
	Hillside	1911 - 1925
8	Southport & Ainsdale	1907
9	Banking & Insurance	1908 - 1941
10	Blundell	1911 - 1935
11	Hillside	1923
12	Southport Municipal	1911
13	Formby Hall	1996

3. 'The Line' 1903.

railway, the view, across the Hillside course, of the nearby clubhouse is a reminder of its distinguished presence. Southport's Hesketh Golf Club lies at the mouth of the Ribble Estuary, to the north of the railway's town centre terminus. Geography might suggest its exclusion from this story. History, however, demands the opposite.

This cluster of courses has been described as ". . . the Mecca of golf".[2] The clubs have justifiably attained an international reputation: both Southport and Ainsdale and Royal Birkdale have hosted Ryder Cup matches with the United States; Royal Birkdale is a regular venue for the Open Championship; whilst all the links have for many years staged major championships and representative matches, both amateur and professional.

South-west Lancashire boasts the largest, and arguably the finest, tract of coastal sand dunes in the country. The strip is over ten miles long and a mile in depth. Sand dunes are only found adjoining gently shelving beaches. In Lancashire, large areas of sand are exposed at low tide and the prevailing south-westerly winds blow the sun-dried sand inland to form a sand dune system. On the large outer hills marram grass, locally called 'starr', struggles to stabilize them, but the cover is not complete and the wind can quickly reshape these 'mobile' dunes. Further inland the dunes become completely covered by

4. Young 'Mobile' Sand Dunes.

6

5. Dune Heath at Ainsdale. The Blundell Golf Course was later laid out on the heath land beyond the fenced railway.

vegetation. Lime, derived from shells, helps promote plant growth. The dunes provided an ideal habitat for rabbits, particularly the inner more mature dunes where other grasses join the starr to give a denser vegetation cover. The deep soft sand was ideal for burrowing. Rabbits from these extensive warrens were systematically farmed. Nature ensured a plentiful supply, with rabbits breeding several times each season and producing up to eight young in each litter.

Where the vegetation cover is thin, the wind can form deep hollows, down to the water table. Initially these hollows, or 'slacks', are wet all the year round. Many later build up to form dry slacks, which are still damp enough to sustain abundant plant life. Further inland dune heath develops. Here the soil has been impoverished by rain leaching down such nutrients that the sand did contain. Local farmers developed special techniques to cultivate the poor soil of this marginal land. Nevertheless the agricultural yields were much inferior to those obtained on the rich black peaty soils of the immediate hinterland. This dune coast did, however, offer ideal sites for golf courses and for houses. Despite biblical warnings against the dangers of building on sand, it does provide excellent dry foundations, which are not subject to the expansion and contraction which occur in clay soils.

Although the coast provides such attractive potential golfing country, this alone is not sufficient to explain the presence of so many golf clubs. This book attempts to trace how the south-west Lancashire coast got its golf courses. It is the story of the pioneers who founded these clubs, the role of the landowners and the railway company, a contribution from the local authority, and – a dimension perhaps understandably neglected in the excellent individual club histories – the crucial inter-relationships between the clubs in the early years. Golf in this area is placed in its social, economic and spatial setting. It is argued that golf was not merely a response to changes in this area but one of the engines of change.

To understand how the Northern Line came to be flanked by so many golf courses it is helpful to trace the nineteenth century development of Liverpool's high-class residential suburbs. Like other cities, it spawned suburbs for the comfort of its wealthier residents. Many great mansions were initially to be found on the slopes of Everton above the city. In 1830 a resident described how:

> ". . . the slopes of the brow, and the platform crest are studded over with beautiful villas and elegant mansions, where the wealthy children of the commerce of Liverpool and the retired gentry and their families live." [3]

Convenience and its commanding position made Everton Hill a fashionable residential suburb of great potential. It was, however, also a site with limitations: the prevailing south-westerly winds passed over Liverpool before reaching Everton. Thus it was ". . . frequently enveloped in dense murky vapours which the crowded dwellings and factories of Liverpool send forth." Perhaps even more potent than the smoke was the inexorable spread of the town itself. The relentless sprawl of people-teeming terraces led the middle classes to abandon such sites and to move to more distant suburbs to the north and south of the city, which offered them the social seclusion they sought. The prospect of turning agricultural land into more profitable high-class residential suburbs led to competition from the landowners to attract such development.

The nineteenth century middle classes had also discovered the attraction of landscape. To the south of the city, gardeners provided parks, such as Prince's and Sefton, as a focus for residential development, whilst to the north the Mersey offered the attractions of sea and sand backed by panoramic views of North Wales. At Bootle the sandy shore was soon ". . . studded with pretty marine villas".[4] They were ". . . residences of importance . . . surrounded by park-like grounds."[5] The new residents included Muspratt, a manufacturer of soda and father of Merseyside's chemical industry. He had ". . . a pleasant villa residence" on the north shore.[6] Arthur Forwood, a wealthy broker, had a garden which ". . . ran down to the seashore".[7]

A little further north John Gladstone, father of the future prime minister, and a successful Liverpool merchant with a spacious house in Rodney Street, had chosen this relatively uninhabited district, well outside the town, where he could live as a landed gentleman. He called it Seaforth, after his wife's family clan. It was ". . . five miles from the Liverpool Exchange", and ". . . the sands, delicious for riding, were one absolute solitude."[8] Gladstone had built 'Seaforth House' in 1815 and actively encouraged further development. Forwood moved from Bootle, which was threatened by the northward's advance of the docks and the mean housing they brought with them, to Seaforth which he described as a ". . . prettily wooded village". Muspratt made the same move and his son later recalled that it was then an isolated place where ". . . most people kept some kind of carriage."

To the north, along the estuary, Crosby and Formby remained small isolated agricultural villages, inland of the sand dunes. The dunes were described by a member of one of the landowning families as:

"A sea boundary belt between the mouth of the Mersey and mouth of the Ribble, a boundary belt peculiar in its nature, and impassible but to the foot of man or horse and forming an elbow of land apart from any communication between town and town; unvisited, untrodden, and, by the general public uncared for and mostly unknown – a desolate and barren tract; a desert (do you say?) an unprofitable waste?"[9]

Further north still, some twenty miles from Liverpool, rural life had been disrupted by the rapid growth amongst barren sand-hills of the seaside resort of Southport, a development fuelled by the canal link with inland Lancashire. Midway through the century the building of a railway between Liverpool and Southport was to transform this coastal area.

It is significant that two major promoters of the Liverpool, Crosby and Southport Railway were the landowners who owned most of the land between Crosby and Southport. They were William Blundell of Crosby Hall, Little Crosby, whose estates included land at Crosby and Hightown, and Thomas Weld-Blundell of nearby Ince Blundell, whose estates included parts of Formby and all of Ainsdale and Birkdale. Indeed, William Blundell was Chairman of the Railway Company, whilst Weld-Blundell had been Chairman of a rival company, before transferring his support. A Parliamentary Bill for the Liverpool, Crosby and Southport Railway received royal assent in 1847. The landowners over whose land the projected railway was routed gave the necessary land, hardly an act of disinterested philanthropy. Despite a severe economic depression, the project went ahead. The route, along the sandy coastal strip, provided no problems of gradient, or foundations, and a single major bridge over the River Alt was required. Consequently the line was completed within a three-month period and was opened in 1848, when the locomotive 'Sefton' pulled a carriage from Waterloo, the temporary southern terminus, to Southport. This modest railway local line, contemptuously dubbed "the shrimp line" by other railway companies, enabled competition to be offered to the well-established southern suburbs of Liverpool, which were linked to the centre by tramway.[10] The day after the opening of the line the *Liverpool Mercury* reported:

> "We hope ere long to see the land along the railway, studded with beautiful villas, surrounded by modest foliage in which 'the merchant princes' . . . may spend their leisure hours in some ease and retirement."[11]

John Sumner, writing in an 1849 Guide Book, suggested that:

> ". . . the whole line of coast, by this railway, offers the most pleasing and tempting allurements for . . . buildings, which, there is little doubt will be seized upon with avidity."[12]

Despite these optimistic forecasts, early high-class residential suburbs were largely restricted to Birkdale. Attempts to replicate this development at Crosby and at Formby initially met with only limited success.

Shortly after the railway's opening, Henry Grazebrook wrote a light-hearted account of a journey from Liverpool to Southport – *Lights along the Line*, a title from which *Links along the Line* is derived. He described the land between Crosby and Birkdale as being ". . . the model on which Zahara, or the great Desert of Africa, was formed." He went on to aver that: "Rabbits and Windmills are the only animals which can exist in this inhospitable region."[13] Even less complimentary was the view of the novelist Nathaniel Hawthorne, then the American Consul in Liverpool. Living in Southport he used the *Line* frequently, and, in 1865, he wrote that although the railway skirted the sea he was ". . . shut from the sight of it by the low sandhills which seem to have been heaped up by the waves. I have not seen a drearier landscape even in Lancashire."[14]

How different was the view of Bernard Darwin, the doyen of golf writers, when he travelled this *Line* in 1922.

> "There is nothing like a range of noble sandhills to set the heart of the average golfer leaping with excitement . . . For almost the whole of the journey between Liverpool and Southport we are kept looking out of the window and plotting miraculous golf courses in our heads. There are four very well known ones, West Lancashire, Formby, Ainsdale and Birkdale, although this last we cannot see from the train; there are two or three others of lesser fame, and there is scope for plenty more. On every side the hills seem to be tossing their sandy heads, as far as the eye can reach."[15]

Henry Longhust later described the area as ". . . that sandy paradise which stretches for miles along the coast between Liverpool and Southport."[16]

Succeeding chapters will plot how each of the golf clubs along the *Line* came into being. The stories of clubs which have not survived, but are part of the area's golfing heritage, are also explored. Further chapters are devoted to the participation of ladies, an early development on this coast; the widening of golf's social base with artisan clubs and municipal courses; and finally, a contemplative look back from the comfort of the 'nineteenth hole', where an attempt is made to draw some conclusions from this historical journey along the *Line*.

REFERENCES

(1) For the early history of Royal Liverpool Golf Club see: Beherend, J. *John Ball of Hoylake* (1989), Farrar, G.B. *The Royal Liverpool Golf Club: A History 1869–1932* (1933) & Beherend, J. *The Story of the Amateur Golf Championship 1885–1995* (1995).

(2) An anonymous quotation in Bailey, F.A. *History of Southport* (1955), p.203.

(3) Syers, R. *The History of Everton* (1830), p.3.

(4) mss. Forwood, W.B. *Bootle Village in Olden Times, A Reminiscence* (undated).

(5) Directory of *Bootle-cum-Linacre* (1888), p.6.

(6) Muspratt, E.K. *My Life and Work* (1917), p.4.

(7) Forwood, W.B. *Some Recollections of a Busy Life* (1910), p.5.

(8) Morley, J. *The Life of William Ewart Gladstone, vol.1.* (1903), p.15.

(9) *The Formbys of Formby* (1910), unpaginated.

(10) Graham, J.W. *Seaport to Seaside: Lines to Southport and Ormskirk* (1985), p.20.

(11) *Liverpool Mercury* 25 July 1848.

(12) Sumner, J. *A Guide to Southport and the Surrounding Neighbourhood and Parish* (1849).

(13) Grazebrook, H. *Lights along the Line: a geographical and topographical description of the salubrious city of Southport* (1855), p.11.

(14) Hawthorne, N. *English Notebooks, vol.2.* (1883), p.343.

(15) Darwin, B. *Country Life* (1922), quoted in Bailey, F.A. op. cit., (1955), p.203.

(16) Longhurst, H. & Cousins, G. *The Ryder Cup 1965* (1965), p.21.

CHAPTER TWO

THE WEST LANCASHIRE GOLF CLUB 1873

"The Southport railway, by its frequent trains, promotes the extension of these places."
Blower, B. & Stonehouse, J. *Liverpool, History of the Mersey and the Streets of Liverpool.* 1870.

William Blundell of Little Crosby, the major landowner and Lord of the Manor of Crosby, was the Chairman of the Liverpool, Crosby and Southport Railway. He hoped that the advent of the railway would open up his thinly populated agricultural estate for commuters to Liverpool. Following his death in 1854, shortly after the opening of the *Line*, the Estate passed to his son Colonel Nicholas Blundell.

The expansion of the dock system through Bootle was pushing the residential suburbs northwards along the Mersey. Muspratt, the chemical manufacturer living at 'Seaforth Hall', close to the boundary with Bootle, observed that ". . . the city has crept up to our garden wall".[1] Land at Seaforth was in the hands of a number of owners, thus when one sold a plot the nature of the subsequent development on it could have a domino effect on adjoining plots or property. After John Gladstone decided to return to Scotland he was unable to find a new tenant for his 'Seaforth House', and he sold some of his land for urban development, including small cheap houses for "the labouring class". Seaforth, the exclusive residential suburb, was being overtaken by "urban sprawl accelerated by Gladstone's initiative."[2] The coming of the railway led to further accretion of cramped working-class terraces close to the station, and Seaforth changed in character from being a place of high-class country residences to a densely populated dormitory for workers.

It appears that the original intention was to bring the railway line from Seaforth, through Waterloo to the old villages of Great Crosby and Little Crosby. This 'inland' route was successfully opposed by landowner William Blundell, the Chairman of the Liverpool, Crosby and Southport Railway Company, who offered the Company the necessary land for the railway, free of cost, on the condition that the line was brought not through the existing settlements, which were on his land, but through his empty sandhills. It was in these sandhills, on the seaward side of the railway, that an important middle-class suburb emerged. Earlier, with the exception of the warren-keeper's cottage, there was no house of any kind on this barren coastal strip until Hightown lighthouse was reached. James Grant, the author and former pupil at Merchant Taylors' School, Crosby, described the area as ". . . the wild moor or common . . . a huge silent rabbit warren."[3] It was in this area that Nicholas Blundell set about developing a high-class residential suburb, which quickly became known as Blundellsands. The first lease was signed in 1854, shortly after his father's death.

"Mr Arnold Baruchson (formerly of Seaforth) built a large house on the sea-front, and this was the beginning of Blundellsands. Other large houses followed . . . The splendid air and the magnificent views quickly made Blundellsands an attractive place, but it had no roads, only sandy lanes, and the approach road was the circuitous one through Crosby."[4]

This account was given by William (later Sir William) Forwood, a wealthy Liverpool broker, whose family provide an example of upper middle-class migration through Liverpool's suburbs. They had moved from Edge Hill to the river front at Bootle until, driven by the advancing docks, they joined the middle-class flight to Seaforth. Later, to escape this area's social decline, they moved south to Sefton Park. The development of Blundellsands then attracted them back to the northern coastal strip, in 1871.

Blundellsands enjoyed the features essential to the success of a high-class residential suburb. Its riverside site was naturally blessed with magnificent views across the estuary, whilst the on-shore prevailing south-westerly winds ensured an unpolluted atmosphere. The railway afforded excellent access. The *Line* also provided an inland barrier, whilst the absence of a road linking Blundellsands to Waterloo in the south contributed to the suburb's much valued privacy and social seclusion. Significantly, a contemporary plan shows a gate on the road linking Blundellsands to Great Crosby. The ownership of the land by a single individual enabled Colonel Blundell to preserve the exclusive nature of this high-class residential area, by imposing covenants on the leases. The site did have some limitations; it was very exposed to the wind, and later changes in the channel, where the River Alt entered the Mersey, led to the sea destroying several of the sea-front mansions.

The 1861 Census Returns show only five properties in Blundellsands. The occupants were a merchant, a shipowner, two agents and a broker. Despite this slow start, Nicholas Blundell made efforts to repeat the residential success achieved by Thomas Weld-Blundell in Birkdale. He employed the Liverpool architects who had made the plan of Birkdale Park for Weld-Blundell and their similar design for Blundellsands was centred on a wide, gently curving road – The Serpentine. As in Birkdale, the roads were asphalted to give a much quieter surface than the ubiquitous cobbles of the city. A newspaper cutting, placed in Nicholas Blundell's diary in the mid 1860s, suggests that the new roads ". . . have given a great impetus to the building of ornamental and first class residences, almost daily springing up in the locality."[5] Such statements were probably part of the developer's 'hype' which included the publication of plans showing the designer's vision for Blundellsands.

Initially Nicholas had sold leases through his brother and his agent. Later, in 1873, he attempted to accelerate development and raise instant capital by selling a block of land to the Liverpool Alliance Land Company for over £10,000. Although this Company took a further eleven plots at the sparsely populated northern end of Blundellsands, the relationship between the landowner and this Company was to prove far from harmonious. Nevertheless, Blundellsands continued to grow. The residents of such a middle-class suburb would expect to have their own church, and in 1874 St Nicholas's was built to fill this need.

6. Villas on The Serpentine, Blundellsands.

A year earlier, in 1873, a golf club, an amenity which was to come to characterise the suburbs of the Northern Line, was formed. A meeting of seven gentlemen was held in Seaforth.[6] These pioneers, no doubt inspired by the success of the Royal Liverpool Golf Club at Hoylake, initially intended to develop a course at Seaforth. It must be remembered that the bricks and mortar that now cover Seaforth were laid on land formerly occupied by sand-hills, and at this time there was still much land, away from the station, that was unbuilt. The area was, however, already experiencing social decline and the 32 founder members accepted Colonel Nicholas Blundell's offer of alternative land on his property at Blundellsands. The land was just inland of the railway at the relatively undeveloped northern end of Blundellsands. This decision was closely followed by the opening of a new station at Hall Road in 1874. After a brief and financially troubled life, the local Liverpool, Crosby and Southport Railway Company had been taken over, in 1855, by the regional Lancashire and Yorkshire Railway Company, thus decreasing the influence of the landowner over the *Line*. It is said that the Hall Road station was built as a result of an initiative by Joseph Gardener, a wealthy resident, who lived at this northern end of Blundellsands and thus faced a long walk to the existing station, which was situated at the southern end of Blundellsands. The Railway Company, which was loathe to add stations which would add to the journey time without producing adequate income, initially declined Gardener's request for a further station stating that another five houses would have to be built in this area before consideration could be given. Mr Gardener duly had them built and obtained his station.[7]

Hall Road Station certainly helped to promote Blundellsands, it was also ideally situated to serve the new golf course. The frequent service gave excellent access to the course from the city. Many of the early members were from Liverpool's strong Scottish community, which figured prominently in the city's commercial life. Members resident in Blundellsands included William (later Sir William) Forwood of 'Rameleh', Burbo Bank, and his neighbour J.F. Caroe, a corn merchant. Other members – brokers, merchants, sugar refiners, shipowners and ship builders – lived in Liverpool's prosperous southern suburbs. An article published in *The Field* in June 1874, reported that: "The clubhouse has been well supported by members of the Hoylake Club and at present has forty-five members."[8] The Club history suggests that many of the early members were involved with both clubs.[9] Members who were also members of the Royal Liverpool Club included the shipowning brothers, Alexander and Lawrence Stoddart (the latter subsequently moved to Blundellsands) and John Dun, a Liverpool banker. All three were accomplished golfers, and Dun was a successful competitor with a string of victories in Royal Liverpool's major competitions. He played as an amateur in that Club's Professional Competition of 1872, and was also the donor of its Dun Challenge

Cross. A captain of Royal Liverpool, his name is still remembered there, at the sixteenth hole. He was also a member of the famous Westward Ho! Club in Devon.

The railway enabled the new golf club to attract a regional membership, and it adopted the name of The West Lancashire Golf Club. It is interesting to note that for a very brief period, in 1870, the Royal Liverpool Club had chosen to use a title reflecting the width of its catchment area – the West Lancashire and Cheshire Golf Club.

The West Lancashire Club attempted to recruit James Morris from the Royal Liverpool Club as its professional. The West Lancashire Club Council Minutes of the 11th May 1874 record that Morris ". . . approved of the way in which the holes had been placed and thought that it would make a good course." He did not, however, accept the post which was filled by David Lowe, also from Hoylake. Lowe was paid a salary of £26 per annum and was allowed to charge members a shilling (5p) a round for playing with him. The 1874 article in *The Field* states that the course was of only nine holes at that time, whilst the Club's centenary publication suggests that the course was always one of eighteen holes. Initially the course was all on the relatively flat land on the inland side of the *Line*. The author of the article in *The Field* described it as being ". . . rather rough, but the general opinion is, that a little play over it will make it a very

7. The Clubhouse and Members, 1888.

16

8. The 1893 Clubhouse. The photograph shows players putting out on the eighteenth green.

good green." The first hole was played in the direction of Liverpool across the ground now occupied by the Waterloo Rugby Football Club. The third hole brought the players back in a northerly direction, past the clubhouse and out into the country beyond Hall Road Station, as far as Sniggery Crossing. The view inland was pastoral, across the fields to the village of Little Crosby. Situated inland of 'The Warren', the grass was much lusher than the closely cropped links at Hoylake. It required frequent cutting and yielded a rich hay crop. In 1884, the Summer Meeting had to be postponed because the grass was too long!

In 1885, West Lancashire was one of the 24 clubs which supported the Royal and Ancient Golf Club in establishing the Amateur Championship. West Lancashire subscribed the sum of five guineas (£5.25) towards the cost of the Championship Cup. The initiative for the Championship came from Royal Liverpool, whose members had been influential in the formation of The West Lancashire Golf Club. Furthermore, the two clubs continued to share a number of members. Undoubtedly, the most distinguished joint member was Harold Hilton, twice winner of the Open, four times the Amateur Champion, and one of the few Englishmen to win the American Amateur Championship. Hilton won many competitions at West Lancashire and later became the Club's first

17

stipendiary secretary. He also served as the first editor of *Golf Monthly* when it was launched in 1911. As will be seen in later chapters, West Lancashire was to enjoy close links with the other clubs along the *Line*, and the toast to "kindred clubs" was regularly made at its annual dinner, which was held at the Alexandra Hotel in Dale Street, Liverpool. More land was leased from the Blundell Estate in 1878 in order to build a modest pavilion, which cost some £361. It was only after an impressive replacement was built in 1893, however, that the Club was able to host its own major functions.

The presence of a large number of Scottish members continued to be a feature of the The West Lancashire Club. Representation from the auld country was so strong that the Club was able to stage 'International' matches with over twenty players a side. Further evidence of West Lancashire's continuing complement of expatriates and its close links with the Liverpool business community was later supplied when the Liverpool Corn Exchange promoted an 'International' foursomes competition for Club members.

Links with the Blundells, from whom the Club leased the course, were good. The senior male member of the family served as President, whilst other

9. *The Footbridge over 'The Line'. The footbridge, which stood by the present eleventh green, was being used as a grandstand in 1927.*

10. Driving from the Tenth Tee. This was one of the new holes in the sandhills on the seaward side of 'The Line'. The building in the background was the long departed Fort Crosby.

Blundells were popular and active members of the Club. The relationship between the Estate and Club appears to have been cordial as the continuing prosperity of the golf club had a beneficial effect on the development of Blundellsands. It was in order to release land to the Estate for building, in 1894, that the Club lost the land at the southern extremity of the course in exchange for land on 'The Warren', on the seaward side of the *Line*. Golfers had to cross the railway on a footbridge in order to play six of the holes, but the reward was to be on true links land. The opportunity was taken to remodel the inland portion of the course and relieve the congestion of holes close to the clubhouse. The labour-intensive nature of greenkeeping, and the cheap cost of such labour, was demonstrated by the size of the staff. There were twelve greenkeepers present at the annual party in 1909, when they all received a gift of tobacco and a pipe from the Club.

An article in the *Crosby Herald* in 1908 emphasised the socially exclusive nature of Blundellsands:

"The houses erected on this portion of the Blundellsands estate are necessarily large and substantial. The residential character of the township is strictly preserved . . . although no hard and fast line is drawn builders must spend between £1000 and £1200 on each house, or

£1800 on a pair. These are of course minimum not maximum charges, and the result is that Blundellsands, from the station to Hall Road, consists of little else but large and palatial residences for Liverpool's commercial and professional men."[10]

An indicator of social status in the nineteenth century was the number of resident servants kept. The majority of houses in Blundellsands had at least two servants, with some containing as many as seven. A Southport newspaper noted the relationship between this growing suburb and the golf club, reporting that golfers of both sexes were "numerous amongst the residents of Blundellsands."[11] A report on the Club's Annual General Meeting in 1908 observed that the Club "serves in a special degree as the non-political club to an already and still rapidly expanding residential district with which it is associated."[12]

With the clubhouse situated close to Hall Road Station, The West Lancashire Golf Club also continued to cater for members living outside the neighbour-

11. The Course, aerial view 1990s.

20

hood. It was claimed that it offered ". . . exceptional facilities to city members." It was partially for the convenience of such members that the Sunday play issue was raised. At a time when Sunday observance was a widely accepted social norm the matter was not easily resolved, and was a vexed question throughout the 1890s. Although there was some illicit playing, it was 1908 before a narrow majority of members voted to sanction Sunday play, and even then it was restricted to members and their personal guests. Interestingly, as at Formby, caddies were not to be employed on Sundays.

As will be seen in a later chapter the West Lancashire ladies had their own course on 'The Warren', immediately to the north of Hall Road Station. After World War II, local demand for building land meant that the Blundell Estate wanted further land from the men's course, close to Hall Road Station. Amalgamation with the Ladies' Club, enabled West Lancashire to preserve 'The Warren' for golf, whilst losing all the holes inland of the railway, along with the cavernous Victorian clubhouse. Such a major change involved the laying out of a virtually new eighteen-hole course. Advantage was taken of the terrain to ensure that West Lancashire would have true seaside links, and that some of the tees would afford vistas across the estuary. In addition to obtaining an

12. The 1962 Clubhouse.

21

enhanced links course a new highly functional clubhouse, to accommodate both ladies and gentlemen, was built in 1962 close to Hall Road Station, at what is now the southern extremity of the course. Befitting its position close to the estuary of the Mersey the building has a slightly nautical air and a balcony from which members can look out across the course and the Mersey. The clubhouse is also able to accommodate major Club social functions. Members financed the building with readily subscribed debentures.

REFERENCES

(1) Muspratt, E.K. *My Life and Work* (1917), p.10.
(2) Checkland, S.G. *The Gladstones: A Family Biography 1784–1851* (1971), p.375.
(3) Luft, H.M. *A History of Merchant Taylors' School Crosby, 1620–1970* (1970), p.139.
(4) Forwood, W.B. *Some Recollections of a Busy Life* (1910), p.117.
(5) Quoted in Hull, R.C. *Social Differentiation in a North Liverpool Suburb: The Case of Great Crosby and Waterloo* (1989), M.A. (Liverpool).
(6) Edwards, L. *The West Lancashire Golf Club, Blundellsands* (1973). This small booklet was published to mark the Club's centenary.
(7) Bolger, P. *Merseyside and District Railway Stations* (1994), p.18.
(8) *The Field* 11 July 1874.
(9) Lowe, F. *The West Lancashire Golf Club: A Slice of Golfing History* (1992), p.5.
(10) Quoted in Hull, R.C. *op. cit.*
(11) *Southport Visiter* 14 April 1908. Note the idiosyncratic spelling of Visiter. Hereafter *S.V.*
(12) *S.V.* 8 December 1908.

CHAPTER THREE

FORMBY GOLF CLUB 1884

"Latterly this success has been aided by the improved railway service, but the first impetus for building and to advanced value of land for residential sites sprang from the formation and development of the Golf Club. Here (Formby) as at other points along the line, the connection between the links and the rise of new villas is very marked. At Hall Road, Freshfield, Birkdale and Southport alike, the landowners are reaping a benefit from the popularity of golf. That the railway company share in this gain has been acknowledged by various concessions."

Report of Formby Golf Club A.G.M., *Southport Visiter* 7 February 1905.

Prior to the coming of the railway *Line* in 1848, Formby was a small agricultural village surrounded by thinly populated farming country. Situated at the shoulder of the Mersey Estuary, Formby was subject to the twin threats of erosion of the coastal sand-hills by the sea and inundation further inland by blown sand. Local farmers had developed a specialised form of husbandry to cope with the unusual conditions. This included the successful cultivation of the local delicacy – asparagus. In 1851, Formby and Ainsdale had a combined population of only 1594. There were two Lords of the Manor, who were the major landowners: the Formby Family, who lived locally and held much of the land around the ancient village; and Thomas Weld-Blundell of Ince-Blundell, whose holding included a large tract of agricultural land to the north of Formby village. Weld-Blundell also owned the adjoining Township of Ainsdale and the Township of Birkdale.

The arrival of the railway brought little initial acceleration in the rate of growth of Formby. The old village was inland of the railway and an early traveller on the *Line* described it as ". . . a calm retreat".[1] An unsuccessful attempt was made to create an exclusive high-class residential district, detached from the village on the seaward side of the new Formby Station. In an attempt to promote this venture, St. Luke's Church was opened in 1855. The consecration programme declared that: "A great increase in population is expected to take place, especially if proper church accommodation is provided."[2] These high hopes were not fulfilled. The modest amount of development that occurred in Formby happened nearer to the railway station, while St. Luke's Church remained an isolated 'folly' amongst the sand dunes.

More significant for the future of golf in Formby was the opening, in 1854, of Freshfield Station, to the north of Formby. Thomas Weld-Blundell appreciated the importance of the railway for residential development and he was able to persuade the Liverpool, Crosby and Southport Railway to open this additional station on his undeveloped land. The fact that he had been one of the principal promoters of this small local railway company probably explains why the Company agreed to this request. Several large mansions were built close to the new station, and it appears that the railway company encouraged this early development by issuing free train passes.[3]

There were further abortive attempts to accelerate residential development in Formby. In 1875, a group of Southport business men launched a company, with £50,000 of capital, and put forward an ambitious plan for a new town – 'Formby-on-Sea', while further north Weld-Blundell proposed a similar scheme for 'Freshfield-on-Sea'. Despite the failure of these schemes Formby enjoyed a steady growth in population as Liverpool men of commerce chose to settle there, but this was the result of gradual accretion around the old village and close to the railway stations. By 1891 the population had risen to just under 6000, and Freshfield, in particular, had become a largely middle-class commuter suburb. It lay on either side of the railway station, with Victoria Road as its spine. As in Blundellsands, the suburb had been established by Liverpool merchants, who lived in substantial villas with large gardens in which they and their families were served by small armies of resident servants.

With the growth of this middle-class suburb, at a time when golf was becoming a fashionable sport on Merseyside, and having fine potential golfing country on the doorstep, Formby Golf Club was a case of a golf club waiting to happen. It was brought into being by the initiative of John Bushby, who called a meeting of ten potential members on the 11th December 1884. The majority of them were brokers or merchants living in Freshfield, but the group also included a local surgeon and the manager of an insurance office. The meeting was chaired by William McIver, a member of the West Lancashire Club. It was decided to form a golf club, limited to 25 Formby residents, and to rent some fields from a local farmer for winter golf only. These decisions were in line with those made by similar groups in many parts of the country: a number of friends coming together to play the newly fashionable Royal and Ancient Game when summer sports were out of season and the middle classes were not indulging their passion for travel.

The ground that they rented was part of the holding of William Halewood, a tenant of Weld-Blundell. As at Hall Road, this marginal land was known as 'The Warren', and William McIver had previously held the shooting rights. Lying to the west of the railway line and immediately to the north of Freshfield Station, 'The Warren' was a flat area and included land that was earlier a part of Weld-Blundell's 'Freshfield-on-Sea' proposal. A payment of £10 for a season of a little over six months was made to Halewood. At that rate, it is highly probable that he was delighted to allow a few golfers to co-exist alongside his stock and crops. Halewood had attended the original meeting and he was made an honorary life member of the new Club. Unfortunately he did not have long to enjoy this privilege: he died shortly after it was granted, as a result of a railway accident on the *Line*.

The terrain and vegetation on 'The Warren' proved to be perfect for the golfers. With the exception of one hole they were able to form the greens without having to lay any turf. One of the pioneers recalled that though the nine holes "... were a bit short, yet to us they appeared very long; for with one

13. Freshfield Station, Looking North. The Formby Golf Club course lies behind the station buildings on the left.

25

or two exceptions we were all duffers; most of us had never handled a club before."[4] The course surrounded some of Halewood's land, which was still cultivated by his widow. Consequently, the Club suffered the tensions experienced by all clubs who have fields of crops adjoining their course. Balls, which cost up to two shillings (10p) each, were an expensive item and not to be lightly discarded when they had been hit over the low banks, locally called 'cops', which surrounded the fields.

Not surprisingly, the tramping of crops by golfers in search of balls was not appreciated by the farmer. The Club had 22 original members, with McIver, one of the few experienced players, becoming the first Captain. The Club's first President was Richard Formby jnr., of Shorrock Hill. He was not the landowner of 'The Warren', but was a member of the family of Formby's other Lord of the Manor. Unlike Weld-Blundell, however, he lived in the community and was involved in it.

A rough thatched wooden hut served as a pavilion for this small group of local golfers. In the following year the Club decided to allow the number of members to be increased to 40, and it was ruled that they would not need to be residents of Formby. Remarkably for such a small, young and inexperienced club, Formby was one of the 24 original clubs which supported and subscribed to the Royal and Ancient Golf Club, in order to set up the Amateur Golf Championship in 1885. The institution of this competition had been suggested by The Royal Liverpool Club and supported by Formby's neighbour – The West Lancashire Golf Club. Members of both of these clubs were playing companions and business associates of Formby members and probably encouraged Formby's participation. It has subsequently been a source of some amusement to members of The West Lancashire Club that the minutes of The Royal and Ancient Golf Club show an asterisk alongside the record of Formby's subscription.[5] The footnote reveals that the pledged guinea (£1.05) had not been paid by January 1887! In the following year the Club extended its rental of the links to cover the whole year. The golfing 'bug' had bitten in Formby. The Club briefly employed a Scottish professional recommended by Old Tom Morris. He was replaced by Peter McEwan, a member of the family of prominent golfers from Musselborough.

Taking advantage of the *Line*, Formby Club arranged matches with West Lancashire, whose experienced team was initially too strong for them, and Southport, whom Formby managed to beat. Inter-club matches became a regular feature. They were played in mid-week, and held twice a year. Business commitments did not appear to press Liverpool's commercial princes too hard in the nineteenth century. Such matches were not the extent of the inter-club contacts, as there was a high incidence of men who were members of more than one of the local clubs. In one match between Formby and West Lancashire, in the 1890s, it was claimed that most of the players in each team were also members of the other club. This plurality of membership was particularly common with the lower handicap players, who competed for the club medals up and down the *Line*.

14. The Present Clubhouse from across 'The Line'.

A good example was John Dun, a Captain of Royal Liverpool and a founder member of both the West Lancashire and Southport Clubs, who also played at Formby. Another distinguished local golfer was Colonel G.F. Smith, an English international and Lancashire champion. In addition to being a member of Formby, he was a very active member of the Royal Liverpool, West Lancashire, Southport and Birkdale Clubs. His name appears on the honours boards of all these clubs. "Niblick", writing in the *Liverpool Courier* in September 1910, suggested that:

> "It is rumoured that periodically Mr Smith presents Mrs Smith with a belt comprised of the scratch medals he has won at the various clubs. The Formby medals are especially covetable, being of a design quite unique."

Perhaps the best known of the *Line's* golfing nomads were Royal Liverpool's great Open Champions John Ball and Harold Hilton. The latter, although secretary at The West Lancashire Golf Club, played much of his golf at Formby. At Formby there was a President's Cup for competition amongst members of neighbouring clubs.

Nevertheless, after five years of existence the Formby membership had not topped the 100 mark. Then in 1891, everything changed. The national and regional popularity of the game was in ascendance. Formby had progressed beyond the situation where leasing land from a local tenant farmer met the golfing needs of a few local residents. It was in this year that the Club negotiated a new lease with the energetic new landowner Charles Weld-Blundell, who had succeeded his father Thomas in 1888. The lease, as amended in 1894, was for the relatively long period of 30 years. The rent to be paid was to be proportionate to the number of members in the Club. The land included the existing course plus further flat ground parallel to the railway. A new 6,000 yard eighteen-hole course was laid out. Despite the relative lack of hills, the course acquired a good reputation. Charles Weld-Blundell, the Lord of the Manor and the landowner from whom the course was now leased, was made Club President. Strangely he held the office for only four years. After his resignation the position remained unfilled for over a decade. To meet the Club's new aspirations a magnificent brick-built clubhouse was erected. In addition to a clubroom and locker room, the building provided a drawing-room, dining-room, and billiard-room. Perhaps most significantly it contained 'dormy' accommodation, including six bedrooms, for visiting golfers.

Formby, with an ever-growing reputation for its course and amenities, was very accessible to Liverpool residents by rail, the clubhouse being hard by Freshfield Station. In addition, the new clubhouse afforded residential facilities for members from inland Lancashire to come and play at the seaside, particularly at the weekends. In 1891 a resident member paid a fee of £1-11-6d (£1.57), whilst non-residents were encouraged with a reduced fee of £1-1s (£1.05). The entrance fee of £1-1s (£1.05) was raised to £3-3s (£3.15) in the following year. In 1891, the Club accepted 179 new members. A new era had dawned in Formby and by the end of the decade the membership stood at over 500. Of all the golf clubs along the *Line*, Formby, with the smallest neighbourhood population, probably owes more of its success to the railway than any of the others. The privilege of golfers' tickets enabled golfers ". . . to complete the journey to and from the links, for the payment of a fare and a quarter."[6] The only justification for a midday express from Liverpool to Formby appears to be for the convenience of golfers. An entry in the Club's Minute Book serves to emphasize this point.

". . . that Marshallsay (the caddie master) be instructed to be at his window on arrival of the 12.30 express from Liverpool. Today he was in McEwan's (the professional) shop, and members had to wait to book caddies."[7]

In the year following the opening of the new clubhouse, the issue of Sunday golf became very contentious. An Editorial in the *Southport Visiter* campaigned hard against this development:

"We deem it our duty to protest most strongly against Sunday golf which is being indulged in weekly at Formby. The Sabbath desecration is the work of a powerful, an organised, and presumably wealthy club, since the members have been able to lease fine hills running to four miles in length and to build a spacious pavilion, clubhouse, or whatever the structure may be called, which affords hotel accommodation to the golfers from a distance, who come to Formby on Saturday night and remain till Monday morning in order that they may spend the Sabbath day in playing golf."[8]

The Club twice debated the issue, and a majority voted for the retention of Sunday play. The *Manchester Guardian* later published a long satirical article commending the Formby links as a tonic for tired business men. It compared the golfing challenge presented by the genuine hazards of Formby with those "manufactured" on Lancashire's inland courses.[9]

A measure of the Club's developing status was that in 1899 the newly formed Oxford and Cambridge Golfing Society initiated a series of matches with the Formby Club, which, incidentally, helped to foster the playing of foursomes within the Club. The visiting team for the inaugural match included Bernard Darwin, whilst later matches featured many distinguished amateur golfers.[10]

The steady progress of the Club was jolted when the clubhouse was destroyed by a nocturnal fire in 1899. The 'kindred' clubs along the *Line* all offered the use of

Oxford and Cambridge Golfing Society v. Formby Golf Club 1899.
Standing, left to right : B. Darwin, G. R. Cox, E. J. P. Magor, A. Rathbone, J. E. Pearson, A. Chisholm, J. Hornby, R. Talbot-Fair, C. Hutchings, J. W. B. Pease, H. C. Ellis, A. H. Crosfield, J. B. Arkle, T. Stone.
Seated, left to right : P. A. Lushington, P. W. Leathart, J. S. Scott, H. C. Colt, P. J. T. Henery, E. H. Buckland, F. P. le Marchand, J. L. Low, A. C. M. Croome, F. M. Dixon, H. Parker, A. C. Robertson, W. A. Henderson, A. P. Dobell, H. H. Hilton.

15. Oxford & Cambridge Golfing Society v Formby Golf Club 1899. This group outside the old clubhouse included Bernard Darwin, the distinguished golf writer, standing on the extreme left, and Harold Hilton, the Open Champion, sitting on the extreme right.

16. Clubhouse Fire 1899.

their facilities to the Formby members, but the Club was able to secure the temporary use of a large villa, in adjoining Victoria Road. The Club took the opportunity to replace the ruined building with a bigger and better clubhouse, which included dormy house accommodation for nine golfers. The speed with which the members raised the required £7,000, through debentures, was an indication of their financial standing. In 1901 the annual membership fee had risen to £3-3s (£3.15), whilst the entrance fee had rocketed to £15-15s (£15.75). Reflecting the Club's escalating social status, Lord Stanley, the son of Lancashire's premier Earl, was the Captain for the opening of the magnificent new building in 1901.

Change came on the course as well: between 1905 and 1907 it was reconstructed to use new ground among the sand-hills. Although demanding more preparation than the flatter original links, the Club was to be rewarded for the work with a truly scenic dune land course. It was about this time that this coast also acquired the coniferous trees, which have become such a feature of the Formby links. A strongly held conviction amongst the current Formby members is that the landowner, Charles Weld-Blundell, planted the trees because his young daughter had a chest condition, in the belief that the trees were beneficial to her health. No evidence has been found to support this contention, certainly, the family seldom stayed in the north west and when they did it was at Ince

Blundell Hall, some distance from the therapeutic vapours of Freshfield's pine woods. Charles Weld-Blundell's purpose in planting these trees was not cosmetic either. In his book *What's Wrong with England*, he described:

> "The provision of wide belts not less than seventy to eighty yards in width, defending the intending farms or holdings from the prevailing winds, and if by the sea, sheltering growing plants from the destructive effect of saline winds." [11]

The landowner had been inspired by the example of plantations he had seen when on holiday on France's Atlantic coast. The Club initially feared that the planting was interfering with the links, but later signalled its acceptance of the trees by adopting the pine as a logo. Another less successful French-inspired initiative was Weld-Blundell's attempt to develop oyster beds on the beach. Over two million oysters were imported from the Bay of Biscay and laid down. Unfortunately they rapidly vanished as the strong current scoured them away, and the Club dining-room lost a potential local delicacy to accompany the renowned Formby asparagus on the menu. The battle between land and sea continues to be played out at Formby and an abandoned tee, close to the previously advancing shore line, presently reminds us of the ever-changing nature of this coastal sand dune system. To replace the lost holes, the Club recently built a string of attractive new holes through the pine woods.

17. The New Clubhouse 1910.

31

The increasing prosperity of the Club coincided with further suburban growth at Freshfield. Large mansions costing £12,000, with annual rentals of about £100, had been built alongside the course in Victoria Road.[12] Nevertheless the continuing importance of out-of-district members was emphasised by the Captain, when speaking at the Annual General Meeting in 1908. Harold Hilton believed that the course deserved more occasional visitors than it received. He wrote "If these links were situated in one of the most inaccessible parts of the kingdom, half of the Golfing world would want to go there every year."[13] An example of the continuing practice of Merseyside golfers joining more than one club was Mr. H. Sutton-Timmis, the Chairman of the Mersey Docks and Harbour Board. Already a member of the Royal Liverpool Golf Club, he joined Formby in 1914 and later he presented a cup for annual competition between the two clubs.

The Club secured a new 30 year lease in 1912. Later in order to accommodate the building of Shireburn Road, to the north of Victoria Road, the Club lost its famous seventeenth hole. This development, at the southern boundary of the course, hastened a reconstruction of the links, on which James Braid, the famous Scottish designer of so many of the British Isles' golf courses, advised the Club. The fee of a few pounds which Braid received for such assignments

18. The Clubhouse 1990s.

was a reflection on the lowly status of professional golfers. A new 25 year lease was signed in the 1930s, when Lord Derby, an active member, was again Captain. He subsequently became President, a position in which he was succeeded by his son, an active participant within the Club and in the wider world of golf. The current Lord Derby continues to serve as the Club President.

A new 50 year lease was signed with Mrs. T. Weld-Blundell in 1946, and the question of the Club buying the links became a live issue. The responsibilities faced by club trustees, where courses are leased, can be frightening. It was the concerns of the Formby trustees about the new lease that precipitated the Club's incorporation as a limited company. The male line of the Weld-Blundells had died out, and in the absence of an active landowner the Club negotiated with the Estate for the purchase of the course. A sum of £24,500 was agreed and loan certificates sold to members quickly raised the necessary funds. Now the owner of its own course, and helped by a substantial legacy from a former member, the Club has been able to continue to develop the course and clubhouse and build the reputation for excellence which Formby Golf Club has deservedly achieved.

As befits a club which was one of the original contributors to the fund to establish The Amateur Championship in 1885, the Formby Club has become closely associated with the amateur game, although it was 1957 before the

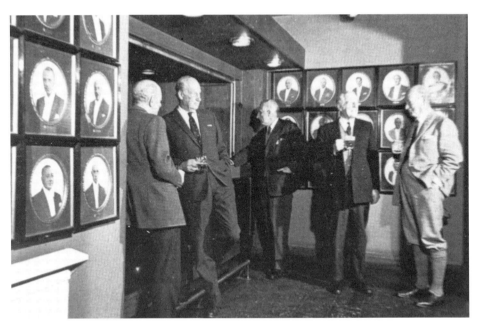

19. The Nineteenth Hole. At the heart of every golf club is a golfer's bar. The Formby Club is renowned for its clubhouse hospitality.

33

Amateur Championship was first played there. This event was due to have been played at Royal St. George's but petrol rationing, following the Suez crisis, caused the Royal and Ancient Golf Club to decide to transfer the event to a club with a railway station close to the course and Formby was chosen. It is ironic that, in the age of the motor car, the railway, which had played such a significant part in the early development of the Formby Club, should have been such a key factor in helping to shape its modern direction. The Championship returned to Formby ten years later, and amongst many other amateur events the Club has hosted have been Home International matches and the Oxford and Cambridge Universities' match. Professional golf has enjoyed only limited exposure at Formby, although more recently the Club has agreed to be one of the qualifying courses for the Open Championship. It is probably not without significance that the Royal and Ancient Golf Club of St. Andrews, which is responsible for the Open Championship, is also responsible for selecting the venues for many of the major amateur events which the Formby Club so values.

REFERENCES

(1) Grazebrook, H. *Lights along the Line: A Geographical and Topographical Description of the Salubrious City of Southport* (1855), p.10.
(2) Beardwood, F. *Notes on the History of Formby* (1970), p.30.
(3) Kelly, E. *The Viking Village: the Story of Formby* (1973), p.75.
(4) Thomas, I.S. *Formby Golf Club 1884–1972* (1972), p.8. This scholarly work gives an excellent account of the beginnings of the Club.
(5) Lowe, F. (Ed.) *The West Lancashire Golf Club: A Slice of Golfing History* (1992), p.7.
(6) Hilton, Harold "Where to Golf" *ABC Guide to the Towns and Pleasure Resorts upon the Lancashire and Yorkshire Railway* (c.1910), p.212.
(7) Thomas, I.S. *op. cit.*, p.25.
(8) *S.V.* 10 December 1892.
(9) *S.V.* 21 March 1905.
(10) Thomas, I.S. *op. cit.*, p.97.
(11) Weld-Blundell, C.J. *What's Wrong with England* (1919), p.111.
(12) *S.V.* 12 August 1899.
(13) Hilton, Harold *op. cit.*, p.212.

CHAPTER FOUR

SOUTHPORT (HESKETH) GOLF CLUB 1885

"Golf since it crossed the border and invaded England bids to be as popular among Englishmen in the future as it has been amongst Scotsmen for the past 400 years. Golf Clubs have within recent years been springing up throughout the country and within the past fortnight, Southport has been added to the list . . . The links will undoubtedly prove a great attraction to golfers in and around Liverpool, being as accessible as Hoylake, and trains run night and morning to assist people residing in Liverpool."

The Field February 1885.

Normally in the nineteenth century, towns in the hands of one or two large landowners were more likely to spawn high-class residential suburbs than was the case in towns where land was held by a number of commercial developers. A single landowner could dictate the overall style of development within an area, exercising control through tight covenants attached to all the leases. On Merseyside, Southport and New Brighton provide a dramatic illustration of the contrast which can result from such patterns of land ownership. Southport, controlled by the Hesketh and Scarisbrick families, was able to attract middle-class residents, who built large red-brick villas in its broad tree-lined roads. From a scattered rural population of about 2,000 at the beginning of the century Southport had become a thriving town of over 40,000 inhabitants by 1891. A government official attributed its success as a dormitory town to the ". . . growing tendency of the upper strata of the commercial world, created and fostered by the general facilities of locomotion, to live away from their business activities." [1] In fact there were as many as sixteen railway stations within the town, probably the highest number for any suburban town of its size in the kingdom. In 1888, a feature writer for the *Liverpool Porcupine* speculated that Southport was "the richest town in the world in proportion to its population."[2] Although such a global accolade probably constituted an exaggeration, it was indicative of the regional significance of Southport.

Most of the early development of Southport had happened in and around the town centre, on Scarisbrick land. The bulk of the Hesketh land was to the north. It consisted of the original village of Churchtown, and the cottages of a scattered fishing and farming community, set in a sea of largely unproductive sand dunes. Charles Hesketh, the landowner, was joint Lord of the Manor and also the Rector. His cautious attitude to the management of his estate had been heavily influenced by the experience of his brother Peter Hesketh Fleetwood who had been financially ruined by his investment in an ambitious scheme to develop his land at Fleetwood. As a result Charles was prepared to take the proceeds of such development as occurred, without being willing to prime the pump by spending on capital schemes.

The Southport Commissioners and private entrepreneurs joined to provide the town with the facilities which the middle classes found attractive. Lord Street was made into an elegant boulevard, and was home to a Library, Art Gallery, Concert Hall, Opera House, Winter Gardens and Aquarium. It was the town's wish to add another amenity which was to transform the fortunes of the Hesketh Estate. In 1865, the local authority had wanted to buy 30 acres of Hesketh's sand-hills for a park. The area, known as "Happy Valley", was a popular venue for outings. It was situated about half a mile beyond the limit of the town's northwards development at the end of Lord Street. The Rector showed himself to be a shrewd business man. He insisted on donating the land to the town. Historians still describe this as a generous philanthropic gesture. The pencil-written minutes of the Park's Committee reveal, however, that as a condition of the gift, he insisted that the authority made a wide crescent-shaped pavement and road around the park. Additionally, the road had to be sewered and connected to the town's still distant sewerage system. This work was done, and thousands of tons of topsoil were imported for the creation of a most attractive park. The effect on the surrounding district was immediate. The plots around the park were quickly taken and filled with large villas. At no expense to the landowner, virtually worthless sand-hills had been transformed into Hesketh Park, the town's most prestigious high-class residential suburb.

A group of wealthy residents from this advantaged area decided to follow the examples already set along the *Line* and establish a golf club. *Southport Golf Club* was founded in January 1885, a few weeks after the Formby Club. Its Foundation Cup acknowledges Captain J. Hardy Welsby as the founder, along with a few of his friends. He was a bachelor and local solicitor who followed his father as registrar of the County Court. His father and brother-in-law were

20. The First Captain and the Professional. This photograph of J. Hardy Welsby and George Strath appears to illustrate something of the nineteenth century relationship between master and man.

amongst the 29 founder members of the Club. J. Hardy Welsby was its first Captain and Honorary Secretary. The founders included Southport's two Lords of the Manor, whose families were the town's principal landowners, and another major Lancashire landowner and his agent. The social status of those on the list can be gauged from the fact that it included two knights and two others who would later become knights, four colonels, a major and a captain. Southport's Town Clerk was also a founder.

A leavening of more experienced golfers came from more distant places. These included John Dun who, as it has been seen, was a founder member of the Royal Liverpool and West Lancashire Golf Clubs, and a member of Formby. From Manchester came another experienced golfer, John MacAlister, a Scotsman residing in Manchester, who had been a founder member of the Manchester St. Andrew's Golf Club, at Manley Park, in 1882, and had been its first Captain. MacAlister was the first of a long list of Manchester members who chose also to be members of Southport. Travelling to an eighteen-hole seaside links course must have been an attractive alternative to playing on their own inland nine-hole course, particularly in the heavy conditions of winter. Hesketh Park had its own station on the Southport to Preston West Lancashire Railway.

The course was situated on the Hesketh Estate's Marshside Hills, to the north of the affluent Hesketh Park area. It had been leased from Colonel Edward Fleetwood Hesketh, who had succeeded his father Charles as Lord of the Manor. Edward was an active founder member and, living at 'The Rookery' in Roe lane, he was a neighbour of J. Hardy Welsby, who lived at 'The Grange'. It seems that Charles had little confidence in his son as a potential manager of the Estate and had left him only ". . . the sandhills, wastes and foreshore", the more valuable property being left to his widow. Bachelor Edward was apparently indifferent to the commercial affairs of the Estate and preferred to indulge his passion for extravagant banquets. He also caused his mother extreme distress when he made an, albeit unsuccessful, attempt to introduce horse-racing to Southport. His parson father had earlier vehemently opposed such a development.

Edward leased some of his land to the Club in 1885, at a nominal rent, and was made a Life President. It appears that his concern was limited to providing his friends with a golf course. Unlike other landowners, he was not motivated by a strong urge to enhance the value of his property. When he died in the following year, at the age of 52, he was the last of the male line and his land reverted to his mother who became the Club's 'Patroness', rather than its President. She was already in her late 70s. Consequently the Club had its links on an estate which was lacking active direction and was left largely in the hands of an agent in Preston.

Despite the low-key approach to the running of the Estate, the members of the Club were men of wealth and position, who quickly secured its future. The original course was of twelve holes. The major sea-wall, the crest of which now provides a public footpath through the course, had not been built, and much of the course was vulnerable to flooding by high spring tides. It was laid out by 'Jof', the second son of 'Old' Tom Morris of St. Andrews. 'Jof' also provided lessons, particularly for the novice golfers. Twenty golfers took part in the first competition on the 14th February 1885. Tom Morris sent a second man with 'Jof', who stayed as the Club professional. He quickly extended the links to a full eighteen holes. The Club had a room in the adjoining New Inn, on Fleetwood Road at the southern, Hesketh Park, end of the course. Although it was only a modest country tavern, the landlord provided lunches for the golfers.

In 1888 the Club moved from its room at the New Inn to a new clubhouse built on the links at the northern, Marshside, end of the course, where there was a railway station nearby at Churchtown. George Strath, of the Fifeshire golfing family, was the new professional, and his wife provided meals in the clubhouse. The *Golfing Annual* for 1888-89 described the putting greens as ". . . the best in England". There is no doubt that such a statement contained a degree of hyperbole, but this claim, and the publication of similar judgements elsewhere, suggest that Strath had the course in good condition.

The Club shared two founder members with Formby, and played its first match with this club. Another founder member was also a West Lancashire member, who distinguished himself in 1890 by winning a monthly medal at Southport in the afternoon, after having been runner-up in the Spring Meeting at Hall Road in the morning. As will be seen in the next chapter, Southport members played a significant role in establishing the Birkdale Club in 1889, and frequent matches were played with this Club. Relationships between the four clubs along the *Line* appear to have been close and cordial. Southport instituted competitions open only to the members of these four, plus golfers from the St. Annes and Manchester clubs. As has been noted, the latter club had a very close association with Southport.

21. *The New Inn, Marshside.*

Mrs Hesketh continued to give the Club the use of the links at a nominal rent and the future of the Club appeared to be secure. At the Annual Meeting in 1891, members were told that the building and furnishing of both the clubhouse and ladies' pavilion had been paid for out of revenue and a surplus was being carried forward. The meeting was also given the startling news that: "In consequence of alterations on the links, the Club had been reluctantly compelled to seek ground elsewhere."[3]

The nature of these alterations is not specified, the Hesketh Estate had no major schemes afoot, and there was so much vacant building land still available in this area that this explanation for a move appears unconvincing. A probable reason lies in the proximity of 'Little Ireland', an area which a Mayor of Southport had earlier described as ". . . the main dark spot on the face of the town."[4] Little Ireland had sprung up in the 1840s. Isolated amidst the wilderness of the Marshside Hills, it was well removed from the town. Only later were the villas of Hesketh Park to spring up between Little Ireland and Southport. The inhabitants of this squalid collection of houses, who were mainly of Irish descent, gained their living as charwomen, cocklers, donkey drivers and rag and bone gatherers. Over 100 people lived there, amidst a

22. Little Ireland.

cluster of pigstyes, hencotes, and stables. Little Ireland gained itself an unsavoury reputation as a rural slum, infamous for drinking and fighting. The address figures prominently in accounts of court cases. Serious assaults and woundings were regular occurrences.[5]

Little Ireland was situated immediately to the south of the links, between them and the outlying mansions of the Hesketh Park district. It seems likely that it was the presence of this settlement that had persuaded the Club to vacate the New Inn, which was patronised by Little Irelanders, and to build its new clubhouse at the north end of the course, well removed from Little Ireland, but also inconveniently distant from the town. The influence of the presence of Little Ireland on the decision to leave the Marshside links was confirmed in a report in 1904 which identified ". . . the contiguity of a block of cottage properties" as one of the reasons.[6]

As well as these negative factors, there was probably a positive impetus for change. The new Club Captain was Charles Scarisbrick, the joint Lord of the Manor and Southport's other major landowner, who would naturally prefer the Club's links to be on his land. The 1891 Annual Meeting was told that:

> "Arrangements are in progress for links between Roe Lane and Blowick, from the Scarisbrick Trustees, where an admirable course of 18 holes can be laid out, with good hazards for about £300, including enlarging and altering the club house."[7]

This suggests that the wooden clubhouse was transferred from Marshside to the new course at Moss Lane. It was curiously claimed that the new course, which measured 5397 yards, was one of the longest in the country. Although it lacked the scenic attraction of the old course, the former agricultural land was quickly put into good order by Strath, and the greens were said to be in excellent condition. The Club had escaped Little Ireland but the golfers were occasionally bothered by smoke from the nearby gasworks at Blowick. During its stay at Moss Lane the Club membership continued to rise, topping 300. The entrance fee was £5-5s (£5.25) and the annual subscription £1-1s (£1.05).

When the Club moved to his land, Charles Scarisbrick became its Patron. Despite this, the link with the Hesketh family was not severed and Mrs Hesketh remained as 'Patroness' until her death in 1898. The Scarisbrick Estate had been trying to extend the Hesketh Park residential development on to its land, which lay further inland. The spine of this middle-class housing was along Roe Lane, which led from the town to the new golf course. The new course was more on the fringe of the town than the old one. It was near a tram line and the Club sought facilities from the Lancashire and Yorkshire Railway for golfers at Blowick Station, on the Southport to Manchester line. Players could alight at Blowick and start their round from the fifth tee, the most distant point from the clubhouse. Nevertheless, Southport Golf Club members living in

23. *The Centenary Medal at Moss Lane 1892.*

42

the Wigan district found the journey long and difficult and in 1898 they played a significant part in founding Wigan Golf Club. In the following year a number of Southport Golf Club members living in the Ormskirk area followed this example and were involved in founding the Ormskirk Club.

In 1901, the Club secured a new fourteen-year lease and was busily involved in improvements to the course, when a dramatic decision to return to the Hesketh links was made. In the year following the Club's removal to Moss Lane the Corporation had condemned most of the property at Little Ireland under the Public Health Act. Sanitation was virtually non-existent. "Three or four only of the houses were provided with privies and these with lock and key attached to the door".[8] Mrs Hesketh chose to evict most of the 'tenants' and demolish the property rather than face the cost of upgrading it. Given the nature of the inhabitants this was a turbulent exercise. Eventually all but half a dozen of the ". . . more respectable families" had been cleared, and the ". . . blot on the landscape", which had cast its shadow over both the golf course and the mansions of nearby Hesketh Park, had been diminished.[9] Mrs. Hesketh gave a further boost to middle-class residential development in the area by erecting the magnificent Emmanuel Church, close to the site of Little Ireland, in Cambridge Road. Donations from three local benefactors, who gave more than £4000, greatly assisted this project.

When Mrs Hesketh died, in her 90s, in 1898, she was succeeded as owner

24. Return to Marshside – Promotional Card 1902.

43

of the Hesketh Estate by her grandson Charles Bibby. Her daughter had married into the Liverpool shipping family. Charles, who also became Lord of the Manor, changed his name, with the permission of Queen Victoria, to Charles Hesketh Bibby. Charles was a young man, and on his return from the South African War he energetically addressed the affairs of the Estate. Recognising the potential value of a golf course as a factor in re-generating interest in villa building in his Hesketh Park Estate, he was the first local landowner prepared to invest in golf. He was proposing a novel arrangement for his new links, which is not unfamiliar in modern contemporary practice. He proposed dual control, between on the one hand himself as the owner and on the other hand the occupiers – a newly formed Hesketh Golf Club. The Hesketh Estate drafted an elaborate 44 page constitution for the Club, which stated that after 60 people had joined they would be able to elect their own committee. The rule that prescribed that residents living on the Hesketh Estate were to receive a twenty percent rebate off their fees highlighted Charles' thinking about the link between golf and middle-class residential development. Interestingly the constitution defined 'residency' as the occupation of a house of not less than £20 net rateable value, thus confirming the Club's middle-class status.

George Lowe, the professional from St. Annes, was engaged to re-lay the course, which had reverted to meadow. Work started in February 1901 and the surrounds and site of Little Ireland, which had nestled amongst the tall dunes, were incorporated into the new course. The former St. Patrick's Catholic School became the greenkeeper's cottage, and the few remaining cottages and buildings were used for the professional, the caddie master, a caddies' shelter, and a bicycle shed for members. Cycling was a popular form of transport with the middle classes. Remnants of some of these buildings can still be seen around the car park. The remains of the track which formed the spine of Little Ireland is still visible, particularly in a dry summer. It runs across the first, seventeenth and eighteenth fairways. Charles also built a clubhouse. The *Liverpool Mercury* described it as being of "manor-house" proportions. Built on a hill, with black and white Tudor facing and a red tile roof, it dominated the skyline of the Ribble Estuary.

The constitution guaranteed any member seven years' play. That is, the proprietor could only discontinue the club seven years after the last admission of a new member. A local newspaper commented:

"It is locally understood that the gift of the site of Hesketh Park was the best investment that the previous Lord of the Manor (the late Rev. Charles Hesketh) made, and it is on the cards that the present owner of the Rookery will through his new links, secure the residential development of his property, which has considerably improved since the erection of Emmanuel Church, between which and the pavilion the golf links lie." [10]

The members of Southport Golf Club, from the modest comfort of their wooden ". . . by no means airy" pavilion, at High Park, cast covetous eyes on the palatial new building. It must have been irksome to think that this and their old seaside links should fall into the hands of others. In the event, notwithstanding the fourteen-year lease which had recently been signed with the Scarisbrick Estate, the Southport Club accepted the "favourable terms" offered by the Hesketh Estate to return to their former links and to be known as the Hesketh Golf Club. The transfer, from Moss Lane, was effected on the first of October 1902. Significantly, Sir Charles Scarisbrick was replaced as Patron by Charles Bibby Hesketh. Like Scarisbrick, who had been Captain of the Club in its first year on his land, so Bibby Hesketh was Captain as the Club returned to Hesketh land. Furthermore, his agent was elected Club Chairman. It appears that after the Club had been abruptly lured back to Hesketh land from Scarisbrick land, Sir Charles Scarisbrick withdrew from the affairs of the Club. He no longer held any office there, thus bringing to an end the era during which both Lords of the Manor had been represented in the Club's hierarchy.

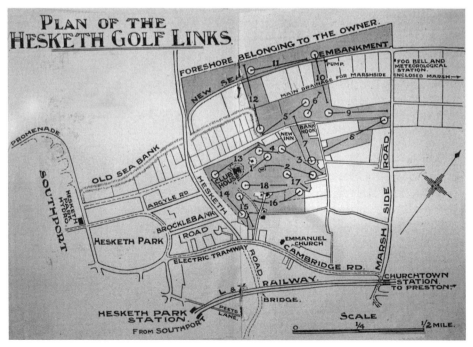

25. Plan of Links and Adjoining Roads 1902.

45

26. *The Clubhouse from the Car Park. The sandhill on the left is protected as a Site of Special Scientific Interest – it is a habitat of the now rare sand lizard.*

By the move, the Southport Club had gained a superbly appointed clubhouse. The first floor contained a club room and balconies from which almost every hole was visible. The new course was superior both to the inland links they had vacated and the original links, which now formed part of it. Fine new holes in the sandhill country around the clubhouse had been added, although the course still extended as far north as Marshside Road. Acceptance of the 1901 constitution, drafted by the Estate, meant that the Club had to surrender much of its autonomy. The Club's income was restricted to what could be made in the 'House', principally the bar profits and the locker rents. Members' fees and visitors' fees went directly to the proprietor.

The Estate also benefited from the boost the presence of a golf club gave to villa building. The *Southport Visiter* described the links as ". . . the proprietary recreation ground, which the landowner has enterprisingly laid out as a most suitable and essentially modern form of developing his building estate."[11] The prime development took place along Hesketh Drive, where the back gardens overlooked the fourteenth (now the fifteenth) hole. A sliced shot could, and still can, find its way into these gardens, all of which had gates giving direct access to the course. It seems, however, that not all of the residents were golf enthusiasts. In December 1909 the *Southport Visiter* published a photograph taken from the course showing two of these gardens. One of them contained a notice stating that: "No balls will be returned", whilst in the neighbouring garden a board proclaimed that "Golfers are allowed to enter this garden".

Control of the Club had passed out of the members' hands. The landowner had been prepared to spend to establish the course, but was less inclined to be generous in its maintenance. Complaints as to the condition of the links became commonplace. The drainage problem which was to blight the outer holes was soon apparent. In the wet winter of 1904, the *Southport Visiter* speculated that ". . . golfers could divide their recreation between punting and skating according to the temperature."[12] Under the existing financial arrangements, the Club Council was reluctant to spend the Club's money to improve the proprietor's course. Not surprisingly, some of the members found these arrangements uncongenial and moved to the Birkdale Club.[13]

27. *The Dining Room c.1904.*

Despite this structural problem, the Club continued to flourish and members played a leading role in the formation of the Lancashire Union of Golf Clubs in 1910. Significantly, the county's big four clubs – West Lancashire, Formby, Birkdale and Lytham – initially refused to join the new Union, fearing that it would attempt to usurp the traditional authority of the Royal and Ancient Golf Club of St. Andrews. The first President of the Lancashire Union was G.F. Smith, a former Captain of the Hesketh Club. It must be remembered that he was also a member of the West Lancashire, Formby and Birkdale clubs. He was succeeded as President by another Hesketh member, J. Raynor Batty. Raynor Batty later became the first President of the newly formed English Golf Union.

Notwithstanding the Club's problems, the course, particularly the holes around the clubhouse, was much admired. Indeed, Harold Hilton wrote of the fourteenth (now the fifteenth):

> "This hole has been eulogised by many as the best in the north of England, while some go further and term it the finest they have ever played in their lives and it is worthy of such praise."[14]

28. *The Course, aerial view 1950s. In the foreground are the gardens of the Hesketh Drive villas.*

29. The Homeopathic Cottage Hospital c.1930. The hospital was built on the old artillery mound. The New Inn was in the trees to the left.

In 1920 the landowner offered the Hesketh Club a fourteen year lease, under which it would take over the entire running of the enterprise. This would involve buying the clubhouse and the equipment used on the course and continuing to pay the Estate a rental for the links. At a special meeting of the Club, which had about 500 members, there was unanimous approval for the Council to proceed with the incorporation of a limited company. All members would take a compulsory £5 share and the fees were more than doubled. Once again master of its own destiny, the Club later spent £2000 on improvements in the clubhouse.

In 1921, the Southport Corporation organised a professional tournament at the Club, the beginning of a continuing relationship with the local golf clubs. The authority had recognised the publicity and tourist value of golf for a seaside resort. In 1926, however, the Estate passed from the hands of the Hesketh family and was sold to a property company. Wanting to realise its assets the Company was proposing to sell the 45 acres of the golf course which lay to the east of Fleetwood Road, which ran through the course, for building. This included not only some of the prime dune land holes but also the

30. The blind drive over Hermon's Hill.

31. Over Hermon's Hill and on the fairway.

30–33. The Fourteenth (now Fifteenth) Hole.

32. Trapped on the blind approach to the green.

33. Finally, putting out.

51

34. "Ahoy There!" on the Seventh Green. The drainage problems on the outer holes were exacerbated by high tides which reached the margins of the course.

clubhouse. The day was saved by the Southport Corporation which was concerned to protect golf as an amenity for the resort, and to implement a town planning strategy which would preserve open space. When the Club's lease was due for renewal, the Southport Corporation joined the Estate in the negotiations and purchased the course in April 1936. The Corporation subsequently offered the Club a 99-year lease, under which the Club was to lose holes to the north of the clubhouse for building land, and to receive in exchange low-lying reclaimed estuary land. The drainage of this new land presented a challenge which continues to exercise the Club. A new sea wall had to be constructed, drainage ditches dug and over 50,000 drain pipes laid. As part of the terms the Club agreed to spend £10,000 in ten years on improving the course and clubhouse, and to pay an increased annual rent of £750.[14] The financial strain such an agreement would place on the Club is self-evident. To help alleviate what amounted to a financial crisis Debenture Bonds, yielding no initial interest were sold to members. Nevertheless, professional championships were soon played on the new links and it was during this period that the extraordinary golfing careers of the two Bentley brothers unfolded. Brought up and attending school in the immediate neighbourhood, they learnt their golf at

Hesketh, and both became English internationals. Harold was amateur champion of England, France, Germany, Italy, and Monte Carlo, and runner-up in the Belgium, Irish and Swedish championships; whilst Arnold was also an English Champion and had the distinction of winning a 1936 Baden-Baden competition run in conjunction with the Berlin Olympics. The Club's future was more permanently secured when, in 1974 immediately prior to local government re-organisation and the absorption of the County Borough of Southport into the Metropolitan Borough of Sefton, the Council allowed the Club to negotiate a new 999-year lease.

The Moss Lane course, vacated in 1902, reverted to pasture before part of it was taken over by the Y.M.C.A. in 1909. It is from this Y.M.C.A. base that the Southport Old Links Golf Club, which still plays this nine-hole course, emerged in 1926. Playing on the links used for a time by the Southport Club, it can claim a minor share in the heritage of the town's senior golf club. Ironically, prior to the formation of the Hesketh Golf Club, there was briefly a club with this name playing on links in Norwood Avenue – Scarisbrick land – about the turn of the century. This short-lived venture had no connection with either the Southport or Hesketh Golf Clubs.

REFERENCES

(1) Committee of Council for Education *Annual Report 1873–1874,* p.81.
(2) Quoted in *Bootle Times* 13 March 1888.
(3) mss. Mitchell,G.E. *Southport Golf Club 1885–1902* (1984). This detailed unpaginated account provided source material for the early years of the Club in: Hick, K. *The Hesketh Golf Club 1885–1985* (1985).
(4) *S.V.* 20 October 1876.
(5) Darwin, C.A. *Southport County Borough Police 1870–1969* (1969), p.23.
(6) Mitchell, G.E. *op. cit.*
(7) *Ibid.*
(8) *S.V.* 31 August 1889.
(9) *S.V.* 8 April 1902.
(10) *S.V.* 14 February 1904.
(11) *Ibid.*
(12) Hilton, Harold "Where to Golf" *ABC Guide to the Towns and Pleasure Resorts upon the Lancashire and Yorkshire Railway* (*c.* 1910), p.218.
(13) Hick, K. *op. cit.,* p.54.
(14) mss. Mitchell, G. *Hesketh Golf Club 1902–1985* (1985).
(15) Hick, K. *op. cit.,* p.110.

CHAPTER FIVE

THE (ROYAL) BIRKDALE
GOLF CLUB 1889

> "It might fairly be claimed that the Golf Club has instituted a new era of development of residential Birkdale, and incited an advance in domestic architecture. The honorary officers of the Club have certainly proved good friends of the landed interest."
>
> *Liverpool Mercury* December 1900.

Despite the rapid growth of Southport during the first half of the nineteenth century, urban development stopped abruptly at the Birkdale boundary. Birkdale was a separate township, owned by a different landowner than Southport – the Blundell family of Ince Blundell. While Southport prospered and grew there was family dissension amongst the Blundells, culminating in a long legal struggle to determine the ownership of the south-west Lancashire estates. Although Birkdale remained a sparsely populated agricultural region, with over half of the township's 2,100 acres being sand-hills and rabbit warrens, its potential value had been greatly increased by the urban development which had occurred in neighbouring Southport.[1]

The family dispute was finally settled in the House of Lords in 1848 and the new owner, Thomas Weld-Blundell, immediately tried to emulate the urban success achieved in Southport. On the last day of September, 1848, the following advertisement appeared in the *Southport Visiter*:

BIRKDALE– The proprietor of the Township of Birkdale has intimated his intention of granting long leases for building purposes on very liberal terms. The land adjoins to Southport, and has a frontage of three miles to the shore. We believe that the township will be laid out under the superintendence of eminent surveyors and landscape gardeners, so that the plan will meet the views as well of those who would wish to possess marine residences of considerable extent as of those who would desire to erect single houses or shops. There is no doubt that this healthy locality will ultimately be covered with elegant and beautiful residences, suitable for the habitation of the most respectable parties.

The chosen site was the sparsely populated hills, west of the railway line, and immediately adjacent to the Southport boundary. The new estate developed away from this boundary. Weld-Blundell called his garden suburb Birkdale Park. As the single landowner he was able to exercise tight control over the type of development which occurred, through the use of restrictive covenants. In 1866, a local guide gave the following description of Birkdale Park:

> "The buildings are generally of a scale of grandeur and magnificence superior to those of Southport, and many are occupied by opulent merchants and manufacturers from Liverpool and Manchester, as well as other wealthy and highly respectable persons."[2]

Birkdale Park was a successful high-class residential suburb, scoring heavily as a healthy location. It also offered social seclusion: the railway provided an inland boundary from the cheaper development that Weld-Blundell had allowed to occur on the other side of the line, whilst in the west and south, the sea and a wilderness of tall sand-hills formed natural barriers. Although a suburb of Southport, the Township of Birkdale had its own local authority. This meant that Birkdale residents were able to share their neighbours' extensive public facilities, without having to pay the higher Southport rates![3] They also enjoyed the town's wealth of private amenities. These included Southport Golf Club, which had a number of members who lived in Birkdale Park.

In 1889, a group got together with the purpose of establishing a golf club in Birkdale. A meeting was held on the 30th July 1889 in the Weld Road home of J.C. Barratt, J.P., a Chairman of the Birkdale Urban District Council. At least three of the nine 'founders' who attended this initial meeting were members of the Southport Club. Charles Weld-Blundell, who had recently inherited the Estate, offered the new club ground inland of the railway, between the centre of agricultural Old Birkdale – The Common – and the expanding working-class dormitory of New Birkdale. Known as Shaw's Hills, the remnants of this course still survive as Bedford Park. It was an area of mature dunes and rough pasture. Although the land was suitable for a golf course the location, close to some very low-value property, might seem to have been an unusual choice. In fact Charles had little alternative as the land west of the *Line*, convenient to Birkdale Park, was not under his sole control. By 1874 Birkdale Park, between the Southport boundary and Oxford Road, had been completely built up, and his father had sold the adjoining 250 acres to the Birkdale Park Land Company. Promoted by Thomas Weld-Blundell, at a time when building in Birkdale Park

35. Shaw's Hills 1930s.

was sluggish, this Company enabled him to raise £5,000 without having to wait for plots to be sold. Ground rent of £6 an acre was payable to him and as a director of the Company he also received director's fees and dividends. Charles was restless to develop his estates and, denied the opportunity to continue in Birkdale Park, he had ambitions for a substantial middle-class residential suburb on land he still owned, around Liverpool Road, inland of the railway. He was probably hoping to use the golf club to help promote this scheme. Mindful of the beneficial influence of the opening of Hesketh Park on residential development in that part of Southport, he also offered land to the local authority for a park in this area. Unlike their Southport counterparts, the Birkdale Council did not want the expense involved in developing and maintaining a park.

The new Club agreed to take the inland site and Weld-Blundell accepted the Presidency. The expense of appointing a professional was no problem for the members, and the Club adopted, with amendments, the Rules of The West Lancashire Golf Club.

The first Honorary Secretary was a Birkdale Park resident, William Shatwell, a solicitor, a local councillor, and a member of the Southport Golf Club. Contemporaries judged him to be the founder of the Birkdale Club.[4] Another Southport member, R.G. Hayward, was the first Captain. Shatwell followed him as Captain, serving for two years. He was succeeded, in 1893, by W.E. Buckley, who was simultaneously Captain of both Birkdale and Southport Golf Clubs! Indeed, nine of Birkdale's first eighteen Captains, and the first two Honorary Secretaries had been, or were still, members of the Southport Club. There were, of course, many others who avoided the limelight of office, and were members of both clubs. When membership lists are examined the link between the two clubs is immediately apparent.[5] As well as 'open' competitions, both clubs held competitions restricted to the members of the two clubs. In 1890, the Honorary Secretary of Southport presented a silver cup to the new Birkdale Club. The two clubs regularly played inter-club matches. Birkdale also enjoyed a close relationship with the West Lancashire and Formby Clubs, but the links were not as extensive as those with Southport. Harold Hilton, Secretary of West Lancashire and a member of Formby, was also a member of Birkdale and, following his success in the Open, was made a life-member.

36. Golf Club Members at Shaw's Hills Course.

37. Portland Hotel c. 1910.

The Shaw's Hills course was some way from the Birkdale Park homes of the majority of the members, and in the absence of a clubhouse they used accommodation at the adjoining Portland Hotel, which was rented at 4s (20p) a week. An account in the *Golfing Annual* of 1889–90 described it as being ten minutes walk from Birkdale Station.[6] The distance was, in fact, a mile. The approach was via Bedford Road, which at this time had not been sewered and was frequently flooded. Even worse, the overflow from the nearby laundry was not efficiently drained, and this nuisance, along with smoke from the laundry's chimney, occasioned frequent complaints in the local papers. In addition, the course had to be reorganised several times owing to the formation of new roads in the district. Not surprisingly, members believed that the insalubrious setting of the course was inhibiting the Club's development. At the annual dinner in April 1894, they were told that the: ". . . grounds were unequal to requirements" and that the Club was actively seeking ". . . an alternative in the most beautiful spot in Birkdale."[7] The land finally chosen was that occupied by the present course, west of the railway. This was Weld-Blundell land immediately south of the block Charles' father had previously sold to the Birkdale Park Land Company.

Negotiations with Weld-Blundell were slow and protracted. In fact, work started on preparing the new course in 1896, although agreement was only finally reached in the following year. The club was allowed the 190-acre site on a peppercorn rent during the first two years, and thereafter charged an annual sum of £100. Although this return was derisory from the landowner's point of view, experience elsewhere had shown that the presence of a golf course had a very beneficial effect on the surrounding property. It acted as a great fertilizer for villa development. Weld-Blundell restricted the Club's lease to 21 years, thus retaining flexibility in relation to the future development of his land.

An interesting insight into how the new location was identified is contained in an account of an obscure court action. In a case at the Liverpool Assizes in 1898 Robert Rimmer, a farmer of Underhill Farm, Birkdale, sought damages from Weld-Blundell for loss of income from his rabbit-warren, on which the new links had been laid out. Rimmer kept cows on Underhill Farm, which was inland of the railway, and it seems that it was this land that Weld-Blundell's agent originally wanted for the golf club's new links. As will be seen later Weld-Blundell had ambitions to link Birkdale to Ainsdale with suburban development along Liverpool Road, which was just inland of this proposed course. In his evidence Rimmer revealed that when the agent offered to re-locate him on another farm, he had argued that he would need compensation for moving and suggested: "Why don't they make their links over the open sandhills where they won't do anyone any harm."[8] This they did. The Club had then, however, gone to great lengths to rid the dunes of rabbits, and Rimmer was successful in his action and received £50 damages. It appears that he might also have contributed to the golf club finding a home which was to become one of the most famous links in the kingdom, when they might have been located on his cow meadows near Windy Harbour Road! A 1908 account of the early years of the Club confirms that ground inland of the railway was inspected and considered.[9]

The Underhill Farm land, an area later occupied by the Southport and Ainsdale course, would have required much less work to transform it into a golf course than was the case across the railway. In the view of a senior member of the Club: "The land which had been chosen as the site of their links was not naturally adapted for that purpose, but rather the contrary."[10] The considerable expense of fashioning a course among the tall dunes did not daunt Birkdale's pioneers, and in order to develop the club the Birkdale Golf Links and Building Company was formed. The course was initially plagued by drainage problems. The grassy hollows between the dunes, known locally as 'slacks', were a delight of wild flowers in the summer, but became shallow lakes in the winter. During the first winter, water made the course impossible to use for some months.[11] An indication of the severity of the flooding, and also of the continuing close relationship with the Southport Golf Club, was the latter's gesture, in December 1897, of electing all the Birkdale members as

38. Slacks amongst the Sand Dunes.

honorary members for the remainder of the winter. It was in the same year that Percy Davies, a member of the Southport Club, donated a handsome silver trophy, to be competed for by teams from the two clubs. Inscribed on the shield are the municipal coat of arms of Southport and that of Weld-Blundell, the Birkdale President. It is interesting to note that the latter was chosen rather than the coat of arms of the Birkdale Urban District Council. Golfers who were members of Birkdale and Southport frequently played in competitions at both courses on the same day. Perhaps the most striking example was on the Whit holiday in 1898, when the same two players came first and second in a 36-hole competition at Southport and an eighteen-hole competition at Birkdale.[12] By September, the new links were such that the Birkdale Club was able to reciprocate the hospitality earlier offered by the Southport Club, and granted all its members honorary membership of Birkdale for a month. By 1898, just over a third of Birkdale's 190 members were shareholders, and £950 had been spent on the links and almost £600 on the clubhouse. The annual subscription had been raised to £1-11-6d (£1.57), whilst the entrance fee was £5-5s (£5.25).

60

It was about this time, after serving for ten years, that Charles Weld-Blundell ceased to be President of Birkdale Golf Club. He was succeeded for a brief period by W.E. Buckley, followed by the long-serving T.O. Clinning. Both were former Captains and Vice-Presidents of the Southport Club and were enthusiastic golfers, who were much more closely involved with the fortunes of the Birkdale Club than had been Weld-Blundell. Nevertheless, it would be interesting to know the reasons for Weld-Blundell's failure to continue as President. He had done the same thing at Formby seven years earlier. As we have seen at the West Lancashire and Hesketh clubs, it was a customary courtesy to bestow this largely nominal title of President on the landowner, from whom a course was leased. An article in *Golfing* in 1899 touched on the relationship between the Birkdale Club and the landowner. The author described the view from the course across some of the yet undeveloped sand dunes.

"Some idea of the natural state of the sandhills may be obtained from this point on looking at the range upon range of sandhills, some of which almost look like Alpine ranges in miniature, some of them being capped with sandhills willow. It is when looking at these sandhills that one is best able to form an opinion as to the value of the land. Ten shillings (50p) an acre does not seem very much, but when it is considered that the Club has to meet

39. Greenkeeper Working on the New Course 1904.

61

the expense of the whole of the work, and there are large tracts on which it is impossible to play, and that the whole of twenty years will see a steady improvement of the land, making it more valuable either for agricultural purposes or for building, it will be seen that the landowner is the gainer in every direction."[13]

Before the formation of the golf course, this tract of infertile Weld-Blundell land lay well beyond the southern limit of housing in Birkdale Park and thus only had value as a rabbit-warren. As well as stimulating building, the Club was improving these hills by installing drainage and importing large quantities of top soil. Significantly, Weld-Blundell had restricted the Club's lease to 21 years. He was, as always, keeping open his commercial options.

The Club was a success and by the turn of the century there were 250 members. A reputation for catering was quickly established; an entry in the Suggestion Book lamented on the absence of the Boar's Head from the Christmas Bill of Fare; while members of the House Committee suffered the ordeal, or delight, of having to sample numerous glasses of port, sherry and liqueur brandy under numbers known only by the Secretary.[14]

Prior to the building of the golf course the nearest houses were still several 100 yards away in Grosvenor Road, on Birkdale Park Land Company plots. The golf correspondent of the *Southport Visiter* claimed that it was the presence of

40. First Clubhouse 1897–1903. This pavilion was situated behind the present fourth green, by the entrance from Lancaster Road.

the golf club that had enabled ". . . the Birkdale Park Land Company to declare a dividend unequalled in its annals."[15] On another occasion he reported that ". . . there is scarcely a home in a large district around the links where at least one member does not reside."[16] A councillor later told a meeting of the Southport Council that: "Numbers of people now resident there would not have come to Birkdale but for the golfing facilities."[17] Members living in the new large villas close to the course included Lt.Col. William MacFie, a wealthy sugar refiner, commander of the local Volunteers, and a founder member of the Southport Golf Club. He lived at nearby 'Lismore' in Waterloo Road, with an establishment of seven resident servants, one of the largest in Birkdale Park. Other local members included Thomas Mulgrew, who lived at the corner of Waterloo and Grosvenor Roads, and George Kilvert, the lard manufacturer, who lived in Trafalgar Road. All three were local councillors, whilst Kilvert and Mulgrew were also major benefactors of the Township's cricket club.

The clubhouse was at the north end of the course, nearest to the built-up area, and was reached from Lancaster Road. Cycling was very fashionable, George Kilvert being one of Birkdale's most enthusiastic cyclists. It appears that the majority of the members cycled to the course, and the Club laid down a cinder track to Lancaster Road for them.[18] For the more lethargic members, however, the local Council licensed three cabs to ply from a new cabstand, ". . . at the corner of Grosvenor Road and Lancaster Road for the convenience of golf players."[19] Unlike the West Lancashire and Formby clubs, Birkdale was some distance from the railway station. Birkdale was principally a club for local residents. The railway served Birkdale residents as commuters rather than as a means of bringing golfers from Liverpool to play at Birkdale.

It transpired that, in error, the Club had built its clubhouse outside the limits of the land which it had leased from Weld-Blundell. In fact it was on Birkdale Park Land Company land. Despite the contribution that the Club had made to the prosperity of this adjoining estate, there was no generosity of spirit and accommodation forthcoming from the Land Company, which now wanted the land for development. In 1904, having been given only very brief notice, the Club was required to demolish its clubhouse.[20] Fearful of the possible migration of members, the Club was anxious to reassure them that there was no threat to the future of the links, and moved quickly to erect a replacement. The new clubhouse, previously a fever hospital in Ormskirk, cost the Club £1,670, a modest sum when compared with the £7000 spent by Formby in 1899. Nevertheless, it was an indication of the sound financial position of the Club. The local paper reported that:

"Well housed before the rigours of winter can supervene, the Birkdale golfers will find cosy quarters in which to reflect during the dark evenings, on the antiquated conditions of the land laws of Old England."[21]

41. Second Clubhouse 1904–1935. The photograph shows members driving from the first (now the fifth) tee. Note the deep drainage ditch in front of the tee.

Birkdale's links were being constantly improved, and soon bore little relationship to the eighteen holes originally laid out. An urgent task was to add length, in recognition of the greater distances the golfers could hit the new rubber-cored balls. Although much improved, the course's early drainage problems had not been completely overcome. The Club's Golden Jubilee publication records that: "Many of the older members of the Club – frequenters of the Birkdale links in the 1909 days – can remember wearing sea boots to wade through the water."[(22)] A further attempt was made to improve the drainage. G.E. Gregson, the Chairman of the Hesketh Golf Club and the agent for the Hesketh Estate, designed the scheme and the Birkdale Club was so pleased with his work that he was made an honorary life member. A contemporary map of Gregson's drainage scheme now hangs in the clubhouse. Later in 1909 the Club was able to successfully host its first major tournament – the Ladies' British Open Match-Play Championship. The close links with the Hesketh Golf Club were again demonstrated with the loan of the Hesketh caddie master and caddies for the duration of the tournament. Unfortunately Birkdale's drainage problems, which stemmed from having used low-lying 'slacks' for fairways, were not completely remedied. Two years later there was a move at the Annual General Meeting to have the subscription reduced because of the waterlogged nature of the course. A 1948 publication of *The Geological Survey of Great Britain* stated that water is commonly met with at shallow depths in the blown sand. This water is known locally as the 'ream'. The survey went on to point out that the Birkdale links had a number of shallow wells, and that water was seen to be standing about four feet below the surface in these after a prolonged period of dry weather.[23] Modern drainage has now eliminated this early curse of the Birkdale links, but the deep ditches serve as a reminder of the damp past.

Meanwhile, Charles Weld-Blundell continued to look for ways to increase the value of his Estate. His grand design was to build up all his land between Birkdale and Formby, and establish a County Borough independent of Southport. The local paper pointed to the lack of security of the golf clubs and their fear of being dispossessed to make way for builders.[24] These fears had substance. Plans from the Weld-Blundell Estate Office show the area of the Birkdale course latticed by projected roads, and the Club's short lease would have allowed an early reversion to the Estate. Fortunately for the Club these ambitious building plans were not realised. The Urban District of Birkdale was amalgamated with Southport, and in his later years Weld-Blundell lost his zeal for direct involvement in the affairs of his Lancashire estates. He spent most of his time in London seeking fulfilment as an author.

42. Approaching Villas c.1912. This photograph of players putting out on the eighteenth (now the fourth) green also shows the approach of the villas in Westbourne Road.

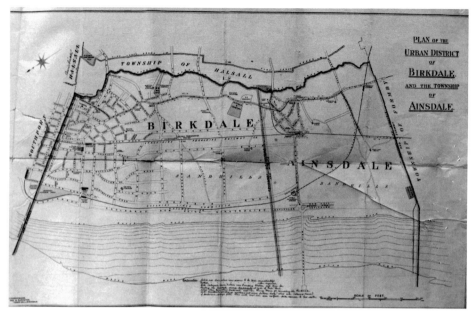

43. Plan Showing Projected Roads Across the Links c.1910.

The Club history reports that in 1922 the Club entered into negotiations with the Estate for the purchase of the course, but that the asking price of £19,000 was considered too high, and a further 21-year lease was accepted.[25] A few years later, however, the course was bought from the Estate by the Southport Corporation. Contemporary fears that the Corporation might have wanted the links for a municipal golf course were misplaced. Southport was attempting to promote itself as a high-class residential resort, and it was believed that a first-class championship golf course would enhance this image. The Corporation was prepared to offer the Club a 99-year lease and in return required a guarantee that the course would be re-modelled and a new clubhouse built, in order that major tournaments could be attracted to the town. The Council appear to have been far-sighted in taking this initiative. Tournament golf was still in its infancy as a major spectator attraction. Prior to 1926 the Royal and Ancient Golf Club had not charged any gate money at the Open Championship, and in that year at Lytham some 12,000 spectators paid £1363 during the three days. In addition to attracting golfing visitors to the town, the Corporation was hoping to attract residents to the adjoining land, on and around Waterloo Road, which it had also bought from the Weld-Blundell Estate.

After years of insecurity as a tenant of Weld-Blundell, with the ever-present threat of losing all or part of the course for building, the Birkdale Club had found a 'Fairy Godmother', with a long-term vision for the links which the members found congenial. A scheme was readily agreed at the Annual General Meeting of 1931, and the systematic development of Birkdale as a major championship venue began. The course was extensively re-modelled on a plan devised by leading golf architects Hawtree and Taylor, the latter was a five times winner of the Open Championship. It was their philosophy of using the valleys of the former slacks as fairways threading between rather than over the sandhills that created Birkdale's championship course. The hills were later to provide natural grandstands for masses of spectators to witness the great golfing spectacles enacted in the arenas below. A new clubhouse was built off Waterloo Road, closer to the new railway station at Hillside. It was strikingly modern, with flat roofs, white stuccoed walls and a tiered tower, and large characteristically curved bay windows. This 1930s style building has been aptly

44. Second Clubhouse – aerial view. The smaller building in the centre of the photograph was the professional's shop, now the artisans' hut. The catering marquees in the background were provided by Woodhead's Restaurant.

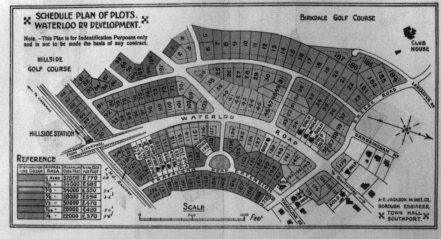

45. *Southport Corporation Building Estate. In addition to buying the course, the Corporation also purchased the surrounding land and attempted to market it for building.*

46. *The Round House, Waterloo Road. Fortunately the Corporation found few purchasers for the plots and Luke Highton's Roundhouse, built in 1924, remained an isolated landmark, whilst the ground between it and the course remained an open space and there was no encroachment of houses onto the course.*

described as resembling ". . . a ship sailing amid a mountainous sea of sand dunes", and so parodied in cartoons.[26] Designed by a local architect, it was claimed, at the opening in 1935, that this was the first clubhouse in Great Britain to be built on these lines. The success of the 1931 scheme was evident when, twenty years later in 1951, the Club was granted its Royal prefix. This was not the result of the links having been played by a member of the Royal family, but rather the recognition of the achievements and status of the Club. One of the principal promoters of the Club's successful attempt to add 'Royal' to its title was not only a senior figure in the Birkdale Club, but also an alderman of the town. The outcome served the interests of both the Club and the Borough. The Club had been due to host its first Open Championship in 1940, but the war was to delay this event for fourteen years. Like Hesketh and Hillside, the Club later benefited from receiving a 999-year lease from the Southport Council, prior to the absorption of Southport into the Metropolitan Borough of Sefton. The prestigious Ryder Cup has been contested on the Birkdale links, which is also a regular venue for the Open Championship. Fortunately the Corporation's plan to develop housing in the Waterloo Road area was not successful. Although some villa building did take place, the open space between Luke Highton's Round House and the links has been preserved.

47. *The New Clubhouse, built 1935.*

48. The Open Championship 1954. The galleries stood surrounding the greens and were able to follow matches around the course.

49. The Open Championship 1976. Stands around the greens transformed the spectators' experience. The Championship now demands ample space for the tented village and car parking.

During the late 1940s and early 1950s, Royal Birkdale was the home club of R.J. (Ronnie) White, arguably the best amateur player of his generation. In a period of American domination of amateur golf, he established an extraordinary record of personal success in Walker Cup matches against the United States. He was also a winner of the English Amateur Championship, and the medal for the most successful amateur in the Open Championship. A solicitor, Ronnie White played in an era when top amateur golfers still had careers outside golf, although even then this involved sacrifices. It was to secure his professional career, and thus his family's future, that he withdrew from the game at a relatively early age.

REFERENCES

(1) For an authoritative account of Birkdale's early history see: Harrop, Sylvia *Old Birkdale and Ainsdale: Life on the south-west Lancashire Coast 1600–1851* (1985).
(2) Mannex, P. *History, Topography and Directory of Mid-Lancashire* (1866), p.246.
(3) See: Foster, Harry *New Birkdale: The Growth of a Lancashire Seaside Suburb 1850–1912* (1995).
(4) *S.V.* 16 May 1908.
(5) mss. Mitchell, G. *Southport Golf Club 1885–1902* (1984). George Mitchell has compiled a list of some 267 nineteenth century members of the Southport Club. Where they are known, he has detailed their associations with other clubs.
(6) Quoted in Johnson, A.J.D. *The Royal Birkdale Golf Club* (1989), p.10. This book devotes several chapters to the early history of the Club, drawing extensively from minute books.
(7) *S.V.* 17 April 1894.
(8) *S.V.* 28 July 1898.
(9) *S.V.* 16 May 1908.
(10) *S.V.* 15 January 1901.
(11) *S.V.* 19 March 1898.
(12) Mitchell, G. *op. cit.*
(13) Quoted in Johnson, A.J.D. *op. cit.*, p.19.
(14) *Ibid.*, p.21.
(15) *S.V.* 2 June 1898.
(16) *S.V.* 23 March 1901.
(17) *S.V.* 7 April 1908.
(18) *S.V.* 20 June 1899.
(19) *S.V.* 3 November 1898.
(20) *S.V.* 13 February 1904.
(21) *S.V.* 17 November 1904.
(22) Anon. *Birkdale Golf Club, Golden Jubilee* (1939).
(23) Geological Survey of Great Britain *Geology of Southport and Formby* (1948), p.43.
(24) *S.V.* 15 May 1909.
(25) Johnson, A.J.D. *op. cit.*, p.32.
(26) *Ibid.*, p.34. An anonymous quotation.

CHAPTER SIX

TWENTIETH CENTURY: SOUTHPORT AND AINSDALE, BLUNDELL, FRESHFIELD, AND HILLSIDE GOLF CLUBS

"Mr. Weld-Blundell has been credited with a natural desire to see a golf club founded at Ainsdale, which, like nothing else, would ensure its rapid development. Given the Lancashire and Yorkshire Railway and Cheshire Lines Railway expresses and a golf course, Manchester and Warrington gentlemen would find Ainsdale a capital golfing place, where golf would give social advantages sought amongst country and seaside residents."

Southport Visiter March 1904.

In the early years of the twentieth century, it seems that the existing four golf clubs along the *Line* were filling up rapidly. The golf correspondent of the *Southport Visiter* wrote of full membership rolls and waiting lists. He chided Weld-Blundell, suggesting that it would be in his interest to have an additional course in Ainsdale. Ainsdale was an agricultural village lying between Birkdale and Formby, where Charles Weld-Blundell was striving to repeat the suburban residential success enjoyed by his father earlier with Birkdale Park. The correspondent pointed to the example of what Charles Hesketh Bibby, the landowner of the Hesketh Estate, had done to promote golf on his land, and what the golfers had done to the benefit of the landowners at Blundellsands, Formby and Birkdale.[1]

A new club – *Grosvenor Golf Club* – did emerge, but it was in Birkdale and not Ainsdale, and was a result of the enterprise of individuals rather than an initiative from the landowner. As he had already demonstrated at Formby and Birkdale, Weld-Blundell was quite prepared to benefit from the presence of a golf course on his land, but he did not want the capital expense involved in preparation. The Grosvenor Club was formed in 1906. F.W. Smith and W. Elliott, the first Captain and Secretary, were both Southport residents, and are not known to have been members of other local golf clubs. The new links lay immediately inland of the *Line*, between it and Birkdale Common. Although on Weld-Blundell land, the small nine-hole course was rented from Peter Lloyd, the tenant of Hillside Farm. The links were well to the south of Birkdale Station, in what is now the Dover Road/Dunkirk Road area. The Club took its name from Grosvenor Road, on the other side of the railway.

The promoters pointed out ". . . that golf in Southport was treated in a serious and expensive manner" and that prior to the opening of the Grosvenor Club:

> ". . . there were two clubs, (Birkdale and Hesketh), whose entrance fees and subscriptions were much in excess of those in other provincial towns, and far in excess of those necessary to maintain a really first-class golf club." [2]

Success for the new club was immediate; after being in existence for only six months, it had 140 members. It demonstrated that there was a local middle-class demand for golf, beyond those who lived in the great villas of Birkdale Park and Hesketh Park. The course was short and rudimentary in character. Pressure, resulting from the increasing number of playing members, caused the committee to consider extending the modest nine-hole course, but the scope to do so was severely constrained by the house-building taking place around the course. It was at this point that the Club received a positive response from the Weld-Blundell Estate. The Committee negotiated for some 100 acres of land between Birkdale and Ainsdale. Lying to the south of the existing course, the projected links, some 6000 yards in length, flanked the railway on its inland edge, and had Liverpool Road, which joined Birkdale and Ainsdale, on the other side. The northern extremity of the course was just south of the Crown Hotel tram terminus.

At a meeting, held at the Temperance Institute in Southport, the members unanimously backed the Committee's recommendation to lease the course. It was announced that the Club would be known as *Southport Golf Club*. This title certainly did not reflect the geographical position of the course, which was well removed from Southport and was situated in a different township – Birkdale. It probably did reflect that many of the early members were from Southport, and that Birkdale was a suburb of Southport. Not surprisingly, the decision to adopt the name of Southport led to ruffled feathers. A member of Hesketh Golf Club wrote to the *Southport Visiter* welcoming the new club, but also pointing out that it was using the name of an old existing club, which had amalgamated with Hesketh. He explained that this was ". . . a flourishing Club with 500 members, famous through the North of England as Hesketh and Southport Golf Club." He accused the new club of acting shabbily, and attempting to appropriate the history and the reputation of the Southport Golf Club.[3] A further extraordinary meeting quickly followed, at which a motion to change the name of the Club, in deference to the wishes of the Hesketh Golf Club, was unanimously carried. The Club was renamed the *Birkdale and Ainsdale Golf Club*, a name which seemed geographically appropriate. Six months later, at the time of the Annual General Meeting, the name had strangely been changed to *Southport and Ainsdale Golf Club*. Ironically, the course was in Birkdale, albeit at the southern end of the township, at the approaches to Ainsdale. It is tempting to believe that while Weld-Blundell would have favoured the inclusion of Ainsdale in the title, he would certainly have preferred it to be coupled with Birkdale, which was also Weld-Blundell land, rather than Southport.

The Club became a limited company, and the course was laid out, at a cost of £440. The plan was drawn up by G. Lowe, the professional at St. Annes, who had recently re-laid the links at Hesketh. The land was less dramatic than Birkdale Golf Club's towering dunes; on the other hand, being inland of the 'slacks', it did not suffer from the same drainage problems and was rarely unfit for play. Converting the partially cultivated land into ". . . thoroughly sporting links", with ". . . natural hazards and splendid land formations", was quickly achieved.[4]

Weld-Blundell was invited to open the course, but was unable to attend and the duties were performed by his agent Mr. Skitt. At the opening ceremony, in June 1907, tributes were paid by the Club Captain to the agent, pointing out that it was due to the ". . . good offices of Mr.Skitt that they had the links on such good terms." Prominent in the formation of the Club had been the two Sugg brothers, former county cricketers who ran a sports' outfitters business. Another of the pioneers was H.D. Gumbley, a director of the Club, after whom the course's famous sixteenth hole is named. This hole, alongside the railway, is dominated by a sleeper-faced bunker set in the face of a large sand ridge, which runs across the fairway.

The Club used its proximity to the *Line* to promote its presence, and placed a ". . . bold advertisement facing the railway."[5] The fee was initially set at two guineas (£2.10) and a limit of 600 was placed on the membership. Over a half of this ambitious total was quickly achieved. The Club entertained the hope that the Lancashire and Yorkshire Railway Company would place a new station between the existing stations at Birkdale and Ainsdale. If this had been done, the Club would have followed the pattern successfully adopted by Formby and West Lancashire of building the clubhouse alongside the station. No station was forthcoming, and by the end of 1908 a new clubhouse had been built at the

50. Southport and Ainsdale Golf Club's First Clubhouse 1909.

northern end of the course. It was linked to Birkdale by tram, the terminus being about a hundred yards north, at the Crown Hotel. Although the course ran alongside the railway, the clubhouse was midway between the Birkdale and Ainsdale stations, but distant from them.

A 'sealed competition' was held to choose a design for the clubhouse. The brief revealed a cautious approach: competitors were asked to design a clubhouse ". . . with a view to be adapted as a pair of villas at some, to be hoped, very distant time."[6] The imposing building provided locker rooms for the gentlemen and ladies, lounges, and ". . . a capacious first floor dining room facing the links." Significantly, it was part of a line of substantial villas built on Liverpool Road at about this time. Here was the beginning of a residential development, which Weld-Blundell wanted to become a continuous belt of property between Birkdale and Ainsdale. The latter had recently been amalgamated into the Urban District of Birkdale. Weld-Blundell offered to give the Council a strip of land to form a pavement. This uncharacteristically generous offer, and his presence when a Council deputation inspected the site, were an indication of his anxiety to secure the development.

Optimism surrounding the move to the new course was quickly tempered by the announcement of a deficit of almost £300 at the 1909 Annual General Meeting. Additional members, with the fee income that they would bring, were urgently needed. The Club's first action was to withdraw the popular 'Free List' under which existing members had been able to invite playing guests. This concession had originally been introduced as a means of advertising.[7] In a dramatic effort to attract new members the entry fee was reduced from £8-8s (£8.40) to only £3-3s (£3.15); a new category of conditional membership was introduced for week day only players; and, unusually for a local golf club, a regular advertisement was placed in the *Southport Visiter*. The annual subscription was raised to two and a half guineas (£2.62) in the following year. The measures taken by the Club appear to have been effective. Over the next two years the deficit was reduced and further improvements were made on the course and in the clubhouse. In negotiations with the Weld-Blundell Estate, the Club was able to extend its lease and to obtain an option on additional land, in the event of parts of the course being required for residential purposes.

The decision to build a clubhouse which could be adapted into a pair of villas proved to be prudent, not because the golf club failed, but because the Club was to lose the north end of its course. This happened in 1922 in order to accommodate the southern extension of Waterloo Road from Grosvenor Road

51. Southport and Ainsdale Golf Club's New Clubhouse, built 1924.

52. Southport and Ainsdale – Driving from the Seventeenth Tee. The telegraph poles mark 'The Line'. Beyond this lies part of the Hillside Golf Club course.

in Birkdale Park to the junction with Liverpool Road. The clubhouse, now well detached from the course, still survives as domestic dwellings – numbers 348 and 350 Liverpool Road. To compensate for the holes lost at the Birkdale end of the course, the option offered by the Estate was exercised and additional land was acquired at the Ainsdale end. A new clubhouse was opened in 1924. Unlike its predecessor, it was situated at the Ainsdale end of the course. As it was less than a quarter of a mile from Ainsdale Station, it was much more convenient for rail passengers. James Braid planned the new course lay-out. Southport and Aindale became a very good test of golf, twice hosting the Ryder Cup Match against the United States of America during the 1930s. The 1933 match, which Great Britain won was attended by:

"... thousands of people who rushed about the course, herded, not always successfully, by volunteer stewards brandishing long poles with pennants at the end, which earned them the name of the 'Southport Lancers'"[8]

On one day over 18,000 spectators paid for admission to the course and uncounted more gatecrashed. This unprecedented attendance was not the

53. Crowds following a game.

54. Play on Gumbleys.

53–55. The Ryder Cup Match 1933.

78

55. The Prince of Wales presents the Ryder Cup.

result of a sudden upsurge in interest, but a reflection of the fact that the event was being watched by the Prince of Wales! Nevertheless, Southport was becoming established as a major venue for tournament golf, and the Ryder Cup match was to return to Southport and Ainsdale in 1937.

The Club also became a prolific nursery for distinguished amateur players. The most famous of these is Dr. David Marsh, an English Amateur Champion, a Captain of a successful Walker Cup team, and more recently a Captain of the Royal and Ancient Golf Club of St Andrews. In 1964 the Club followed the example of Formby Golf Club and raised the money in order to buy its course. Southport and Ainsdale paid in the region of £25,000 to purchase the freehold. This price might appear to be modest for such a tract of land, but planning restrictions no longer allowed the estates the freedom that they had previously enjoyed when they chose to re-possess land for house building. Thus Southport and Ainsdale enjoys the unique distinction, amongst the Southport clubs along the *Line*, of being the owner of its own course.

The old nine-hole Grosvenor course, alongside the railway at Dover Road, was not allowed to lie fallow for long. In July 1907 W.A. Findlay, a Scottish dentist with a Southport town centre practice, rented the course in his own name. The new club was to be known as the *Blundell Golf Club* and the annual fee was set at a guinea (£1.05), only half of the Southport and Ainsdale figure. The first Honorary Secretary was Henry Pidduck, a Lord Street jeweller, perhaps an indication of the commercial background of some of the early members. Only a short walk from Birkdale Station, the Club was to prove very popular with golfers from along the *Line*. In 1902, this heavily-used commuter line was one of the first in the country to be electrified and the time gap between trains was reduced. The Blundell Club advertised the availability of special rail fares for members, with the Secretary providing the necessary vouchers.[9] A newspaper report later indicated that: "Many Liverpool golfers wanting cheap golf have found out the merits of the Blundell Club."[10] This trend was confirmed when the Club was reported to be holding a thirteen-a-side match between members who lived in Southport and those who were Liverpool residents.

Building continued around the nine-hole course and local residents again lobbied the Lancashire and Yorkshire Railway Company to place a station between Birkdale and Ainsdale. It was claimed that there were now 660 houses in the vicinity. All three local golf clubs – Birkdale, Southport and Ainsdale, and Blundell – stood to benefit from the opening of such a conveniently situated station and joined the clamour. It was suggested that the name "Birkdale Links" might be appropriate. Charles Weld-Blundell, the Birkdale Park Land Company, and the Birkdale Urban District Council added their support. The *Line* had become a highly successful commuter link and, the railway company was reluctant to alienate its passengers by adding additional stations and thus increase journey times. The pressure came to nought and it was only after the Waterloo Road extension, including the railway bridge, was built in the 1920s, thus linking the area to prestigious Birkdale Park, that Hillside Station was opened.

The thriving Blundell Club built a new clubhouse in 1907 and in the following year, despite the house-building which had occurred in the district, it managed to acquire several adjacent fields, using this land to lengthen and improve the nine-hole course. The longest hole was extended to 420 yards. During its financial crisis in 1909 the Southport and Ainsdale Club approached the Blundell Club offering it amalgamation. This was an attempt to boost its own membership. The founders of the Blundell Club considered the offer and decided to put it to the members because its lease from Peter Lloyd, who was himself a tenant, was necessarily short compared with that granted by Charles Weld-Blundell to the Southport and Ainsdale Club. Only a minority of the members of this popular but inexpensive club favoured the scheme; it seems that the majority preferred the cheaper golf available in their own Club. The annual fee for the Blundell Club was still only half of that charged by Southport and Ainsdale.

It was only two years later, however, that this small nine-hole course was

56. Blundell Golf Club Clubhouse at Ainsdale 1911.

again to act as the springboard for re-location. In 1911, the Blundell Club moved to a new course, again on Weld-Blundell land, but this time to the south of Ainsdale village. Inland of the railway, the course lay between the *Line* and Liverpool Road, and extended as far south as Pinfold Lane, close to the boundary between Ainsdale and Formby, at Woodvale. Similarly situated to Southport and Ainsdale, on partially cultivated land, the course would have required only modest preparation. The approach to the Club was from Ainsdale village, along Chesterfield Road. Ainsdale was still relatively undeveloped and Liverpool golfers travelling to Ainsdale on the *Line* would have been critical to the Club's success. Great emphasis was placed on the convenience of the new course for Liverpool businessmen, and the first tee and the substantial clubhouse were only a short distance from the end of the platform of Ainsdale Station. One notable member and course-record holder was D.E.B. Soulby, an Irish international and Lancashire Champion. Amongst his many other clubs were Hesketh and Birkdale, where his name appears on the honours' boards.

During the 1920s, the Hillside Club, which was experiencing very severe financial difficulties, followed the earlier example of the Southport and Ainsdale Club and unsuccessfully sought amalgamation with the Blundell

81

Club. Ironically it was the Blundell Club itself which was to disappear in 1935, and the course has since been entirely given over to the bricks and mortar that Weld-Blundell hoped that it would help to attract. It appears probable that the lease had expired as alternative land, nearer to Formby, which was offered by the Estate was refused by the Club. It is possible that the Blundell Club was no longer in a healthy condition. Findlay, the founder, was an active member of the Hesketh Club by this time. The 1930s were a time of economic depression and, as will be seen, there was by that time a surfeit of golf courses in the district.

When the Blundell Club had vacated its old course at Dover Road the site was considered by the Southport Town Council as a location for a Municipal Golf Course. This option was not taken up and there was a fear that the land was to be built-up: 38 residents of nearby Dunkirk Road petitioned that it should be left an open space.[11] In fact, the course later became the home of another new Club – Hillside. The land was again leased from Peter Lloyd of Hillside Farm and the Club decided to use this name in its title. The precise beginnings of *Hillside Golf Club* are shrouded in mystery. Philip Irlam, the

57. Blundell Golf Club – Medals 1918–1919. The shield on the silver Ladies' Medal was enamelled red, whilst that on the men's was blue.

58. Hillside Golf Club – Clubhouse on the Old Course. This pavilion style clubhouse replaced an earlier one-room wooden hut.

historian of the Club, speculates that it was founded at a meeting held at the Portland Hotel in 1911.[12] Unfortunately, none of the earliest records has survived. This gap in the archives is exacerbated by the curious absence of references to a new Hillside Club in the local press. The Grosvenor and Blundell Clubs, which had previously started on this nine-hole course, enthusiastically 'used' the sports' pages as free advertising. If, as is postulated, the Hillside Club was formed and used the course in 1911, the September *Southport Visiter* reports concerning the possibility of house building on this former golf course land, suggest that at the earliest Hillside could not have been active before the latter part of 1911.

The first firm evidence concerning Hillside Golf Club appears to be a membership card from 1913: this indicates a small club as it was limited to only 25 members. The course was still very rough, being grazed by Lloyd's cattle and, as with some contemporary 'country' courses, the greens were protected by fences. From these modest beginnings, Hillside made rapid progress. A one-room wooden hut was replaced by a new two-room clubhouse. The first reported team match was against the Y.M.C.A. Club, which had taken over the abandoned Southport Club links at High Park.

Influential early members of Hillside included: Fred Jackson the first

83

59. Hillside Golf Club – Clubhouse on the New Course.

Secretary and Treasurer, who was a retired railwayman from the regional audit office; Richard Mook the first Captain, who was a grocer; and George Keeley, a clerk in the borough treasurer's office, who was one of the Club's first honorary life members.[13] In 1923 the Club became a limited company with capital of £3,000, and was able to lease land flanking the *Line* on its seaward side. The Weld-Blundell Estate let the Club have 105 acres on a 21 year lease. Initially it used some holes on this new land with some of the old holes in order to make up eighteen. In 1925, a full eighteen-hole course was opened on the new site, whilst the old course, which had been largely surrounded by houses, was built over. The new course was long and narrow, extending south to Ainsdale. It enclosed 'The Hawes', an isolated 17th century farm house situated at the Ainsdale end.

A brick clubhouse, costing £2,400, was built at the northern end of the course close to the new Hillside Station. As with the Southport and Ainsdale Club, the clubhouse was designed to allow for the possibility of its sale as a domestic dwelling, in the case of the Club going into liquidation. Sadly, the extensive and expensive development of the Hillside Club precipitated a financial crisis. In an attempt to recruit further members, the payment of entry fees was suspended, and overtures were made to the Blundell Club seeking amalgamation. In 1926 the Board of Directors resigned en bloc but, with disaster threatening, a new Board was able to steer the Hillside Club into calmer waters. Louis Rowlandson, the new Chairman of the Club, was to hold this office until 1940 and, although he was sometimes judged to be authoritarian in manner and action, the foundation for the Club's prosperous future was laid.

As the fortune of the Club improved, Philip Irlam notes that strong links were forged with its near neighbour Southport and Ainsdale, which flanked the *Line* on the inland side. As part of the Southport Council's policy of preserving open spaces and promoting golf both as a tourist attraction and as a stimulus to housing development, it later bought the Hillside course when the Estate was wanting to sell the lease. Prior to local government re-organisation in 1974, the Southport Corporation extended this lease to 999 years, as it did in the cases of both Royal Birkdale and Hesketh. In 1961, the holes beyond 'The Hawes', at the south end of the course, had been exchanged with the Council for the tall

60. Hillside Golf Club – Driving off the First Tee. The tee was behind the line of the new clubhouse. The new Hillside Railway Station, built in 1924, can be seen on Waterloo Road bridge.

sandhills that lay between the Hillside and Royal Birkdale courses. This new land gave the Club the opportunity to shape its present majestic championship links. The back nine holes, in particular, have attracted much praise including receiving the highest commendation from Greg Norman, the great Australian golfer.

If Birkdale Park had been Thomas Weld-Blundell's suburban "Jewel in the Crown", it was at the relatively undeveloped seaward side of the *Line* at Ainsdale that his son Charles sought to leave his mark. Surviving detailed plans and pictorial panoramic maps reveal the extent of his ambitious schemes for Ainsdale-on-Sea. He envisaged a promenade, pier, gardens, lakes, hotels and other attractions. The promenade would link to Westbourne Road in Birkdale, a step towards his vision of a continuous conurbation, on Weld-Blundell land, which would stretch from the Southport boundary to Formby. Plans from the Estate Office show the dunes latticed with projected roads. He had made several attempts to promote his Ainsdale-on-Sea scheme, but only a handful of large villas, on Station Road, were built. Although he was unable to persuade the Lancashire and Yorkshire Railway to build a station between Birkdale and Ainsdale, Weld-Blundell had made the option of a station at Ainsdale-on-Sea a condition of leasing land for the Southport and Cheshire Lines Extension Railway. This line, which linked Southport to the national rail network, ran through the dunes and behind the Birkdale Golf Club's course, a route now followed by the Coastal Road. Weld-Blundell was able to require this financially impoverished railway company to build Seaside Station, to service Ainsdale-on-Sea, at a cost of some £2,200, (at a time when the returns from the use of the station did not even pay the station master's wages). Weld-Blundell blithely spoke of attracting 10,000 visitors a year to Seaside Station;

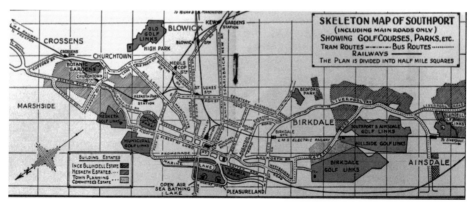

61. Map of Southport, showing Golf Courses c.1930. This map designed to promote building development highlighted the presence of golf clubs.

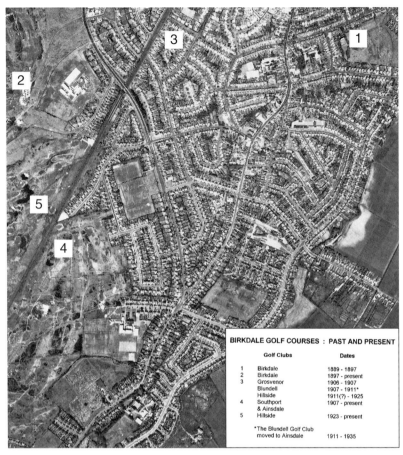

BIRKDALE GOLF COURSES : PAST AND PRESENT		
	Golf Clubs	Dates
1	Birkdale	1889 - 1897
2	Birkdale	1897 - present
3	Grosvenor	1906 - 1907
	Blundell	1907 - 1911*
	Hillside	1911(?) - 1925
4	Southport	1907 - present
	& Ainsdale	
5	Hillside	1923 - present
	*The Blundell Golf Club	
	moved to Ainsdale	1911 - 1935

62. Birkdale Golf Courses, Past and Present – aerial view.

furthermore, he wanted a siding laying down, so that the building materials for the houses, which he envisaged covering the area, could be unloaded.

Encouraged by the evidence of the beneficial influence of the presence of a golf course on suburban development, Weld-Blundell believed that a golf course, between the Lancashire and Yorkshire Railway and Cheshire Lines Railway, would give an impetus to the sluggish rate of residential growth in this area. He had already demonstrated that it was not his policy to become actively involved in the expense of providing golf courses. His problem at Ainsdale was the lack of sufficient local residents to sponsor a course, a shortage exacerbated by the wealth of existing golf provision in the area. Nevertheless, in 1906, it appeared that he had found an unusual prospective tenant to develop a course.

63. Ainsdale-on-Sea Railway Station. The dune area inland of this Southport and Cheshire Lines Extension Railway station was unsuccessfully offered by Weld-Blundell to the Liverpool Banking and Insurance Golf Club.

The Liverpool banking and insurance community had been holding golf competitions locally and were minded to establish their own club. The twelve pioneers were all in business within a 50 yard radius of Liverpool Town Hall. They had 150 promises to join a new club, and a meeting was called at the Exchange Buildings, in Liverpool. It was revealed that the suggested club had the option of securing links at Ainsdale-on-Sea that were virtually a southwards continuation of the links of the Birkdale Golf Club. The meeting was told that there was a recently built hotel alongside the Seaside Station of the Cheshire Lines Railway which could act as headquarters for the club, and the Ainsdale Station of the Lancashire and Yorkshire Railway was only a few minutes walk away. Furthermore, "Satisfactory conditions for season tickets could be arranged with the competing railway companies."[14]

The principal organiser was Fred McLaren, who had acted as Honorary Secretary, chaired the meeting, and had previously negotiated with the Weld-Blundell Estate. At the well-attended meeting, he described the links offered by

Weld-Blundell, ". . . a generous landowner with a zeal for the improvement of his residential estate by the most modern means, the multiplication of golf clubs." The verdict of the majority at the meeting, however, was that the tall scrub-covered dunes presented hazards to daunt the golfing beginners who would constitute the membership of the new club. In addition, there appeared to be evidence of financial caution, possibly a case of the members' corporate banking instincts operating. Perhaps aware of the problems that Birkdale Golf Club was facing at that time, it was suggested that the ". . . drainage and turfage would prove costly beyond the resources of a young club". On these grounds the Ainsdale option, proposed by the organisers, was rejected. Attempts by Weld-Blundell to attract other golfing tenants failed, and these wild dunes have survived as a nature reserve.

A committee was elected and instructed to seek further offers from landowners. Weld-Blundell was still anxious to have this Club on his land. But it was to be 1908 before the *Liverpool Banking and Insurance Golf Club* finally leased land from him, for a course at Freshfield. The land had been the subject of an exchange between Weld-Blundell and Formby's other landowner – the Formby family. Following his normal custom he restricted the Club's lease to 21 years. The 190 acres lay to the north of Freshfield Station, that is between Freshfield and Ainsdale. The course was on the inland side of the *Line*, opposite and parallel to the links of the Formby Golf Club. The land was not unlike the

64. Liverpool Banking and Insurance Golf Club Clubhouse.

partially cultivated land on which the Southport and Ainsdale, Blundell, and West Lancashire links were formed. A former member describes it as ". . . a flat course, with banks and ditches, and some very big bunkers."[15] It was claimed that the eighteen-hole course was the longest in the district. Despite being rebuffed over the Ainsdale-on-Sea course Fred McLaren, who had done so much to bring the Club into being, was appropriately chosen as the inaugural Captain. The business background of the promoters was readily apparent in their early decision to form a limited liability company. The 'entente cordiale', which had characterised the relationships between the golf clubs along the *Line* was again evident: the new Club expressed its appreciation of the goodwill shown by the Formby Club, which offered advice through its Secretary and Professional.

A competition was held for the design of the clubhouse. It resulted in a picturesque two-storey building, which featured a full-length verandah. The large clubroom held over 200 lockers and on the first floor was a dining room.[16] Although not a 'closed' club, the firm membership base in Liverpool's banking and insurance community, and the ease of access via Freshfield Station, ensured the Club's early success. The entrance fee of five guineas (£5.25), was only a third of that of the Formby Club across the *Line*, a half of that charged at Birkdale and Hesketh, and the same as that of Southport and Ainsdale. The Liverpool Banking and Insurance Golf Club depended even more on the railway than did the neighbouring Formby Club, and the absence of local membership proved to be a long-term structural weakness. Support for a regional, 'professionally' based, club dwindled as more and more golf courses were built in the suburbs of Liverpool. The Club later abandoned its restrictive-sounding title and became the *Freshfield Golf Club*. As in other clubs, World War II meant that many members were away on active service. The membership at Freshfield was down to about 40 when, in 1941, the course was requisitioned for conversion into Woodvale aerodrome. Although the clubhouse continued to function, and the members enjoyed the courtesy of the neighbouring Formby courses, the Club petered out. What a boon this course would have been if it had still existed when Freshfield's great building boom came in the 1960s.

The creation of golf clubs along the *Line*, however, has not yet finished. With all the existing clubs being full, there is still a demand for the opportunity to be a member of a golf club. The environmental lobby and the designation of surviving dune land, on the seaward side of the *Line*, as nature reserves, restricts the possibility of additional courses on this prime links land. The creation of new golf courses is not cheap, nevertheless entrepreneurs are stepping into this market and currently building a proprietary golf course centred on old Formby Hall. Ironically, this is immediately inland of the Woodvale airfield, the former site of the Freshfield Club course. Extensive landscaping with the creation of banks and ponds, and the planting of trees has been undertaken in order to transform this relatively flat agricultural land into a golf course.

65. Formby Hall Golf Club 1996. Construction work on clubhouse and course in progress.

REFERENCES

(1) *S.V.* 29 March 1904.
(2) *S.V.* 18 October 1906.
(3) *S.V.* 10 November 1906.
(4) *S.V.* 19 October 1907.
(5) *S.V.* 5 October 1907.
(6) *S.V.* 28 November 1908.
(7) *S.V.* 18 May 1909.
(8) Longhurst, H. & Cousins, G. *The Ryder Cup 1965* (1965), p.8.
(9) *S.V.* 16 September 1907.
(10) *S.V.* 3 November 1908.
(11) *S.V.* 16 September 1911.
(12) Irlam, P. *A Lively Octogenarian: Hillside Golf Club 1911–1991* (1993), p.7.
(13) *Ibid.*, pp.9–14.
(14) *S.V.* 3 July 1906.
(15) Recollections of Mrs. Jean Noble (née Scott) of Formby, who, with her parents, was a member of the Freshfield Club.
(16) *S.V.* 26 September 1908.

CHAPTER SEVEN

LADIES ON THE LINKS

"Constitutionally and physically women are unfitted to golf. The first women's championship will be the last. They are bound to fall out and quarrel on the slightest, or no pretext."

Horace Hutchinson *Letter to the Ladies Golf Union* 1893.

There are historically shadowy claims that Catherine of Aragon, one of Henry VIII's wives, was connected with golf. The evidence relating to Mary Queen of Scots' involvement in the Royal and Ancient Game is much firmer. She was reported to be playing golf an indecent two days after the murder of her husband Lord Darnley! By the 1870s there was a Ladies' Golf Club at St Andrews. An article in the local *Gazette* suggested that ". . . the ladies game was limited only to strokes of the putting variety." However, it seems that before the end of the century: "Some ladies had forsaken the gentility of the putter for strokes that demanded full swings." One commentator suggested that ladies' links

". . . should be laid out on the model, though on a small scale, of the 'long round' containing some short putting holes, some longer holes admitting a drive or two of seventy or eighty yards and a few suitable hazards . . . The postures and gestures of a full swing are not particularly graceful when the player is clad in female dress."[1]

The game was played by Victorian gentlewomen. Contemporary photographs show that whilst playing they wore long skirts reaching down to the ankle, sometimes having a bustle, high-necked blouses, frequently with a club tie, a jacket, and high-buttoned shoes. This ensemble would be topped by a voluminous broad brimmed hat. What the photographs do not show is the extent of the underwear which Victorian ladies customarily wore: camisole, chemise, corset, petticoats, and stockings. The wonder is that so encumbered they could hit the ball at all. It seems that an ingenious American lady invented a device to contain and control flowing skirts in high winds. Known as a "Miss Higgins", it consisted of an elasticated band which was slipped over the folds of the skirt.[2] Strips of leather were frequently sewn around the bottom of the skirt, both to add weight and to prevent fraying. The *Southport Visiter* regularly contained an illustrated advertisement from a Chapel Street draper advocating the use of "Ocean Serge" for ladies' golfing outfits. It is not surprising that many clubs developed separate short courses for women, which took account of the distance that ladies could hit the ball. This is not to suggest that there was sexual apartheid in these early days of golf. There is much evidence that points to men and women playing together, and enjoying cordial relationships within their clubs.

The minutes of the original 1884 meeting of the *Formby Golf Club* include a set of rules. Rule number six states that: "Ladies being relatives of members shall be permitted to use the links, Saturdays and such days as set aside by the Council excepted."[3] Thus restricted in their playing conditions, ladies were only required to pay a half subscription. The records show that from the first season mixed foursomes competitions were played. Early trophies are evidence of the the good relationships between the sexes. There are examples of ladies' trophies being presented by men and vice-versa. In order to protect the turf, the Formby ladies were not allowed to wear the currently fashionable high heeled boots on the course. Less gallantly, the Club Committee passed a rule decreeing that ladies should at all times give way to gentlemen.

In 1886 the ladies were invited to establish their own committee to conduct competitions and oversee handicaps. Ten years later there was a much more significant development: *Formby Ladies' Golf Club* was formed. A nine-hole

66. Formby Ladies' Golf Club – Clubhouse 1996. To the right is the professional's shop and to the rear the Formby Golf Club clubhouse.

course was laid out, on land enclosed within the men's course. Although the longest hole measured only some 300 yards, the par was 82. A single-storied pavilion was built for the Ladies' Club, which ran independently of the men's Club, to which a rent was paid. The parent Club was responsible for the design, preparation and upkeep of the course. The original membership numbered about 120 and, unlike the men, the Ladies' Club did not allow play on Sundays. The inaugural Lancashire Ladies' Championship was played at Formby in 1907. Two years later a new eighteen-hole course was opened. The Club prospered and the clubhouse was enlarged in 1912. During the Formby Golf Club's financially difficult years of World War I, the ladies' course was temporarily reduced to only nine holes in order to save work. The post-war revival in the fortunes of the men's Club was shared by the ladies and, in 1930, the course was host to the Ladies' British Open Amateur Championship. Progress continued and the Club now boasts a testing eighteen-hole course, some 5421 yards long, with a par of 71. The ladies still enjoy their own distinctive and charming clubhouse, which was built on the site of the original pavilion. Their trophies include two donated by Lord Derby and the Countess of Derby, when they were Captains of the men's and ladies' clubs respectively in 1934.

Although the club records show ladies playing golf at Formby as early as 1884, a ladies' golf club was formed in Blundellsands some five years earlier than the Formby Ladies' Golf Club. In 1891 the *West Lancashire Ladies Golf Club* came into being following a meeting of 38 ladies in the Burbo Bank Road home of Mrs F.W. Cornelius. Although not a founder member of the Ladies' Golf Union, West Lancashire Ladies' Club was elected to membership within the first year. The extent of the local demand for ladies' golf was demonstrated by the Blundellsands' Club having as many as 86 Founder Members. By the end of its first year this vigorous infant had 159 members and a further 45 male associates. The first President was Lady Forwood, the wife of a West Lancashire founder member, who lived in Burbo Bank Road.[4] Following Lady Forwood's death in 1896, she was succeeded as President by the Countess of Derby, who was, at this time, a very enthusiastic supporter of the West Lancashire Ladies' Club.

The first course was of nine holes laid out on 'The Warren', on the seaward side of the railway alongside Hall Road West, which the Blundellsand's villa builders had not yet reached. The ladies paid an annual rental of £20, whilst the cost of preparing the course was £12.15s (£12.75). A small modest clubhouse was built close to Hall Road Station. The venture was a success and in 1895 the Ladies' Club laid out a new eighteen-hole course and built a more comfortable clubhouse. It was nearer to the sea than its predecessor and caddie boys were paid 2d to carry a golf bag from the station. Placed over the fireplace in the clubhouse was an ornamental shield listing the Captains.[5] A number of the Club's major trophies, including the Countess of Derby's Vase and the

Staveley-Taylor Challenge Vase, date from these early years. An 1897 publication reported that:

> "The West Lancashire Ladies' Golf Club is the largest in the North of England. It possesses an eighteen hole course of its own, and certainly the clubhouse is far more attractive than that of the average club for ladies."[6]

A decade after its formation the Club had 159 lady members. The West Lancashire Ladies' Club appears to have enjoyed much more autonomy than its counterpart at Formby. In 1902, the *Southport Visiter* described it as being ". . . almost unique in being managed solely by women."[7] Men were admitted, but only as associate members, and a number of these gave the Club professional advice and assumed personal liability in acting as its Trustees. By 1901, this thriving Club had 277 lady members and 134 male associates.

The gradual advance of villa-building in Blundellsands eventually threatened the golf links and in 1909 the sixteenth, seventeenth and eighteenth holes were lost. Significantly, it was one of West Lancashire's lady members who arranged the lease of further land and it was the ladies who were responsible for the laying out of a new course. The ladies of West Lancashire repeatedly demonstrated their capacity to run their own Club. The new 5050 yard-long course, designed for ladies, was described as ". . . one of the finest, if not the finest to be found anywhere."[8] To Harold Hilton the Open Champion, it was an ". . . ideal miniature championship course, but large enough to provide most fair and interesting golf to the hardest hitters of the male sex."[9] The independence of the ladies extended to their Club having its own professional. In 1911 a verandah, overlooking the nine-hole putting green, was added to the clubhouse. The clubhouse had to be enlarged to accommodate the growth in membership: by 1912 the Club was full with 320 full members, 100 conditional members, and 150 associates.[10] These numbers indicate that this was far more than a neighbourhood amenity and the Club had regional significance. The annual subscription for ladies was £2.2s (£2.10), the same as that levied by the Formby Club. By 1930 the course had been stretched to 5,300 yards and Jerry Bond, the Club's professional, set a course record of 60 strokes.

Unlike the men, whose course was on agricultural land inland of the railway, the ladies were on links land, hard by the estuary of the Mersey. Consequently their course was perpetually threatened with inundation by blown sand from the unstabilised outer dunes. Brushwood fences were erected and star grass planted in this unequal battle against nature. The course was not fenced on this seaward side and for many years golf was interrupted by ". . . picnics, boy scouts and even footballers." Appeals to the landowner for a fence were in vain.

As in the men's clubs there were close ties between the ladies' clubs along the *Line*, with regular inter-club matches and open competitions for the

67. West Lancashire Ladies' Golf Club – Clubhouse c.1912. The large villa on the left was 'Brooklyn', which served as the clubhouse from 1947.

members. In the early years the West Lancashire Ladies' team was vastly too strong for that of Formby. Their playing strength was demonstrated by the presence of two West Lancashire ladies in the successful Lancashire County Team.

During World War II the laying of mines on land adjoining the Mersey estuary reduced the course to nine holes, and the ladies' clubhouse was occupied by an army unit, damaged and eventually burned down! After the war, the Blundell Estate wanted the site for further house building. As the Estate also wanted land inland of the railway from the men's Club, the amalgamation of the men's and ladies' Clubs appeared to be the rational way forward. The land from the remnants of the ladies' course and the nine seaward holes of the men's course became the site for West Lancashire's fine new eighteen-hole links. Unfortunately the plan to develop a separate nine-hole ladies' course foundered because of the expense.

Apparently it was 1889 before ladies began to play on the *Southport Golf Club's* course. In the absence of a separate ladies' course, the ladies played from their own forward tees. As at the other clubs, there are records of mixed foursomes being played. A newspaper report in 1890 suggests the existence of a Ladies' Club:

"The Ladies are beginning to play a good game and as soon as they can be placed in their new quarters their Club will no doubt increase more rapidly than it has done since its formation a few months ago."[11]

68. Hesketh Ladies at Moss Lane, pre 1902. This group includes Lottie Cheetham standing second left.

There are no records to indicate that there was an autonomous Southport Ladies' Club at this time. Indeed the evidence suggests that it was a number of years before they were even able to have their own section within the Club. Nevertheless, the ladies had the use of one of the cottages, at the Marshside end of the course, as a clubhouse. There were, and still are, a number of such low-slung thatched cottages in the vicinity of the course. It was in 'The Cottage' that the professional's wife served lunch and afternoon tea to the competitors in the Club's first "Open Competition" in 1891. Members from the Birkdale, West Lancashire, Formby and St. Annes clubs took part. The prize, donated by the Vice-President of the Southport Club, was a gold bracelet in the form of a golf club, with a diamond to represent the golf ball.

In 1892, the Southport Club moved inland to its new course in Moss Lane. The Ladies had their own club rooms at 27/29 Moss Lane. These houses, still in existence, provided a lounge with a balcony overlooking the eighteenth green. As the premises were also equipped with one of the first 'flush toilets' in Southport, all looked to be set fair for the ladies. Notwithstanding these amenities, however, it appears that there was little activity on the part of the Club's lady golfers during the next few years. The new links were not as conveniently sited for access from Southport's residential areas as was the old course, and the terrain would have been damper and heavier underfoot. In addition, as subscriber members only, the ladies were restricted to playing on three days a week.

Birkdale Golf Club granted ladies permission to play in 1889, shortly after the Club's formation. They were given a room in the greenkeeper's house in Bedford Road, which adjoined the course. At the Annual General Meeting in 1890 the following proposal was unanimously carried:

> "That ladies may be elected active members of the Club, . . . but shall not be entitled to play on the links on Saturdays, Bank Holidays, Competition Days or any other days reserved by the Committee."[12]

The Green Committee approved a special course for the ladies. Unusually it was a six-hole course, including five of the nine holes of the men's course, and a further hole near their rooms in the greenkeeper's house. Presumably this exclusively ladies' hole was a short one, which like all the others would be played three times in a round. Birkdale's first course was on an inland site, well removed from the Birkdale Park homes of most of the lady members. The situation was not dissimilar from that obtaining at the new Southport Golf Club course at Moss Lane.

It is at this point that there is some ambiguity about the progress of ladies' golf in Southport. Between 1892 and 1896 there are no records of ladies playing at the Southport Club's Moss Lane course. However, a group calling itself the *Birkdale Palace Ladies' Golf Club* was much in evidence during these four years. The Palace Ladies included members of both the Southport and Birkdale Clubs. It has been conjectured by club historians that these games might have been played on the Birkdale and Southport courses. It appears much more likely that these ladies had chosen to play on a long-departed and now forgotten golf course, which was situated in the spacious grounds of the Palace Hotel.

Birkdale Park's Palace Hotel had been built in 1866 on a 20 acre site. Part of the extensive grounds, which extended as far inland as Lulworth Road, were tastefully laid out and included croquet lawns, bowling greens, an archery field, children's playground, and gardens with walks, bowers, and seats. Local residents could buy contracts to use these facilities. Although the fashionable hotel was very successful as a local social centre, it was unable to consistently attract sufficient residential visitors to be a commercial success.

Although some of its land alongside Weld and Lulworth Roads was sold off for building, the hotel decided to attempt to cash in on the vogue for golf and utilise some of its remaining spare acres of dune land for a course. It must have been modest in size, and was advertised as a "ladies' course". It seems reasonable to assume that it was on this course that the Birkdale Palace Ladies' Golf Club played.[13] Members were drawn from the families of some of Birkdale Park's wealthiest residents. For example, they included Mrs Burton and her two

*69. Birkdale Palace Hotel. This view shows some of the extensive grounds, on which the ladies'
golf course was laid out.*

daughters, who lived very close to the course, in 'The Warren' in Westcliffe Road.
'The Warren', a huge villa, had been built at a cost of £10,000 on a four-acre site.
Another member, Miss Mayall lived nearby at the extensive 'Clairville' in
Lulworth Road. The most successful golfer was probably Lottie Cheetham, one of
three sisters who ran 'Westlands' in Westcliffe Road, one of Birkdale Park's many
expensive private schools for girls. A member of both the Southport and Birkdale
Clubs, she represented the North of England at golf on several occasions.

There does not appear to have been any schism in the Southport and
Birkdale Clubs connected with the setting up of the Birkdale Palace Ladies'
Golf Club. Many of the valuable prizes which were presented to the winners of
the competitions were donated by male officials of the Southport Club. They
included gold brooches and bangles, sometimes inset with precious stones. It
seems likely that the popularity of the new club was a product of the
convenience of its location, its situation in a high-class residential area, the
comforts available in the hotel, and the opportunity to play on a short ladies'
course. There is no doubt that the Club became very fashionable.

Despite these advantages, the new Club did not endure. From 1896, references to its competitions disappear from the local newspapers, and the focus of ladies' golf moved back to the Southport and Birkdale Clubs. One of the last references to the Birkdale Palace Ladies' Golf Club appeared in 1897, when the members held a retirement presentation for Lottie Cheetham. The hotel's advertisements, however, continued to feature the availability of a ladies' golf course, and a newspaper article in the following year reported that there was still a ladies' golf club playing at the Birkdale Palace Hotel, although the club was not named.

Even during the brief years of the Birkdale Palace Ladies' Golf Club, the Birkdale Golf Club ladies had continued to play some competitions on the Club's original Shaw's Hills course. As with the men, the move from insalubrious inland Birkdale to Birkdale Park, in 1897, led to a boost in the number of lady members. The Ladies' Section flourished and soon had an annual list of over 20 fixtures, and by the turn of the century there were 55 members, a modest number when compared with the memberships of the West Lancashire and Formby Clubs. Of course these two clubs were greatly advantaged by having their own ladies' courses. An 1899 edition of *Golfing* suggested that the Birkdale Golf Club was considering building a new clubhouse, and that it was the intention to pass the present clubhouse over for the exclusive use of the ladies, a proposal which did not materialise.[14] A newspaper report in 1904 suggested that few ladies were taking advantage of the opportunity to play on Saturdays.[15] It is interesting to note that the first major tournament played on the Birkdale links was the Ladies' Golf Union's Ladies' British Open Match-Play Championship, in 1909.

The demise of the Birkdale Palace Club also coincided with an upturn in the activities of Southport Ladies. In 1896, the Club held its first recorded ladies' event for four years. It was an Open Meeting, significantly, but inaccurately, described as the Club's "First Open". The competitors included ladies from Formby and West Lancashire but, perhaps oddly, not from Birkdale. As with the men, many ladies were members of more than one of the local clubs. It appears that there were more ladies who were members of both Formby and Southport than there were men. Conversely, it appeared that there were many fewer ladies who were members of Southport and Birkdale than was the case with the men. The possibility of playing on Formby's shorter ladies' course must have been attractive. A further indication of the close ties between the Southport and Formby ladies was the frequency of their inter-club matches. These matches were very decisively won by the Formby Club. There are no records of inter-club matches between the Southport and Birkdale Clubs at this time. At the Southport Club, ladies still appear to have constituted a section of the main Club, rather than being a separate club. In 1896 there were 75 lady members. In 1898 the Club promulgated a notice on etiquette, including this patronising reference to ladies:

70. Driving from the first (now fifth) tee.

71. Putting on the eighteenth (now fourth) green.

70–71. Ladies' Golf Union Ladies' British Open Match-Play Championship –
Birkdale Golf Club 1909.

"If you choose as a partner a woman who keeps you back by slow play, don't quarrel with her on this account. Abide by your choice, and do what you can to help her enjoy the game. Don't appear to prefer your ball to her company, and stand over it while she, some distance off, is making vain efforts to catch up with you. Play near her, and endeavour to make her feel that she is not a such a bad player after all."[16]

When, in 1902, the Southport Club returned to its old links and was reconstituted as the Hesketh Golf Club, the ladies were given a very attractive club-room on the upper floor of the magnificent new clubhouse. Not all the male members approved of this situation. As early as December 1902 there was this entry in the suggestion book: "That the Ladies' Club Room be turned into a Billiard Room, and that the cottage at the back (now the greenkeeper's house) be turned into the ladies' club room."[17] The Ladies' section had a Secretary from 1906, at the latest, and its own Captain from the following year. The annual subscription of £1.1s (£1.05) was half of that at West Lancashire and Formby.

The *Grosvenor* (later *Southport and Ainsdale*) and the *Blundell* Golf Clubs both advertised for the recruitment of lady members during their early years. They offered associate member status, as in the Southport and Birkdale model, rather than the membership of a ladies' golf club as at West Lancashire and Formby.

72. Hillside Golf Club – Ladies' Committee.

The Grosvenor Club charged ladies half fees. Interestingly, they were here allowed to play competitions on Saturdays. One of the most successful lady players in the early years was the teenage daughter of Walter Sugg, the county cricketer. She was also a champion at the currently popular game of 'ping pong' (table tennis). Southport and Ainsdale later had a very active ladies' section. Initially ladies were only allowed to play on Saturdays if they were partnering a man, this rule was rescinded in 1909.[18] There are reports of frequent competitions and inter-club matches, including those with the Birkdale and Formby Clubs. After the Blundell Club moved to its new links in Ainsdale a ladies' committee was formed in 1912. There was also a thriving Ladies' Section attached to the *Liverpool Banking and Insurance Golf Club* (later *Freshfield Golf Club*), unfortunately the records do not appear to have survived. This Club did, however, host the Lancashire Ladies' Championship in 1927. As has been indicated, knowledge of the early history of the *Hillside Golf Club* is sketchy. Philip Irlam suggests that there were ". . . lady members . . . from the start", although little appears to be known about their participation and status until a Ladies' Section was formed in 1920 and the first Captain elected in the following year. This occurred whilst the Club was still using the nine-hole course inland of the railway.

The most distinguished lady golfer to emerge along the *Line* was Royal Birkdale's Frances 'Bunty' Smith (née Stephens). A golfing contemporary of Ronnie White, she won the English Ladies' Championship three times and the British Ladies' Championship twice; played in five Curtis Cup matches against the United States, in which she was never beaten in the singles, and twice successfully faced the responsibility of winning the deciding match. Following a glittering playing career she became an influential figure in the sport, becoming the President of the English Ladies' Golf Union.

Footnote

An anecdote in Ivor Thomas' history of the Formby Club provides an illuminating commentary on prevailing male attitudes towards lady members. The Council Minutes reveal that, about the turn of the century, the Secretary of the Ladies' Club wrote asking for a new set of tee boxes to be bought to replace the existing ones, which were very dilapidated. The Council agreed; but when they arrived, they decided to let the ladies have the best of their old boxes and keep the new ones for the men![19]

REFERENCES

(1) Nickerson, E. *Golf: A Women's History* (1987). See Chapters One and Two.
(2) Mair, L. *One Hundred Years of Women's Golf* (1992), p.42.
(3) Thomas, I. *Formby Golf Club 1884–1972* (1972), p.7. The development of ladies' golf

at Formby is well recognised in Ivor Thomas' history of his Club.

(4) Pratt, N.A. & Dickinson, C.J. *The West Lancashire Ladies' Golf Club: 100 Years of Ladies' Golf 1891–1991* (1991), p.1.

(5) *S.V.* 19 September 1895.

(6) Whitley, M. *Every Girl's Book of Sport Occupation and Pastime* (1897).

(7) *S.V.* 23 December 1902.

(8) *S.V.* 2 February 1909.

(9) Hilton, H. "Where to Golf" *ABC Guide to the Towns and Pleasure Resorts upon the Lancashire and Yorkshire Railway* (*c*.1910), p.238.

(10) *S.V.* 11 June 1912.

(11) Dixon, N. *Hesketh Ladies* (1989), p.6.

(12) Johnson, A.J.D. *The History of the Royal Birkdale Golf Club* (1989), p.12.

(13) *S.V.* See frequent advertisements placed by the Palace Hotel and reports of Club competitions.

(14) Johnson, A.J.D. *op. cit.*, p.14.

(15) *S.V.* 27 December 1904.

(16) Dixon, N. *op. cit.*, p.9.

(17) *Ibid.*, p.11.

(18) *S.V.* 13 May 1909.

(19) Thomas, I. *op. cit.*, p.24.

CHAPTER EIGHT

CADDIES, ARTISAN CLUBS AND MUNICIPAL COURSES

"Why should not something be done to provide golf, as well as bowls, for the working man. I am sure that there are lots who would take it up if they could get it cheaply enough. I don't see why Southport shouldn't have a public golf course like they have in other towns."

A letter to the *Southport Visiter* 1905.

Golf along the *Line* was an expensive middle-class pursuit. Would-be members of golf clubs faced not only an annual subscription, but also a substantial entrance fee, which could be up to five times greater than the annual figure. One of additional costs was the employment of a caddie to carry the golf clubs – about 1s (5p) a round. As well as easing the burden on the golfer, this activity introduced working-class men, boys and girls to the 'Royal and Ancient Game'. Although children under the age of thirteen were not allowed to caddie at St. Andrews, children, rather than men, were favoured as caddies in the Southport district. In 1899, the headmaster of the Birkdale Board School reported that "The system of employing schoolboys for caddies is responsible for much irregularity of some boys."[1] Indeed, on one occasion seventeen boys were absent playing in a tournament, which the golf club had defiantly arranged for them during school hours. The Birkdale Golf Club later co-operated with the school, refusing to employ boys who were still pupils.

Education Committee statistics show that caddying became a popular source of full-time employment for school leavers in Southport. The members regularly provided prizes for competitions played by the young caddies and also an annual dinner. It was concern for the welfare of the young caddies that led the Birkdale Club, in 1908, to propose the formation of *The Birkdale Golf Club Caddie Boys' Association*.[2] As well as providing clothing and boots for the boys, generous backing from Club members enabled the Association to obtain a club house in Brighton Road, where the caddie master, Sergeant Charles Packham, acted as caretaker and supervisor. These premises, where smoking and

73. Boy Caddies at Southport Golf Club Moss Lane 1892. Harold Hilton, the Open Champion, demonstrates his putting stroke.

gambling were forbidden, included a games' room, a gymnasium, and facilities for the boys to have a bath. In addition to leisure activities, the Association had an important commitment to find future employment for the boys. There were workshops at Brighton Road, where the boys were instructed in the trades of boot-making and carpentry. At a time when the local education authority was developing Evening Continuation and Extension Classes, the Caddie Boys' Association clubhouse was recognised as a sub-centre offering classes in gardening (a major source of employment in residential Birkdale), shoemaking, carpentry, cooking and English. There had to be a minimum of ten caddies in each class.[3] In order to encourage self-reliance the boys had to contribute towards the cost of running the Association. The records show that several caddies were successfully helped to obtain further employment, particularly with shipping lines.

In 1909 the West Lancashire Club put on a "Caddies' Supper", with hot-pot, bun-loaf and entertainment, for 140 child caddies; while in the same year Hesketh Golf Club entertained 70 caddies at a similar event. In 1907 the Hesketh Club issued a leaflet – *Instructions to Caddies*. Isette Pearson, the first secretary of the Ladies' Golf Union, was so impressed with this document that she took copies of it to distribute to other golf clubs. Caddies were under the direction of a caddie master and the training of caddies affected their standing and their cost: most local clubs had different rates for First and Second Class Caddies. The tall flag-staff, alongside the Hesketh clubhouse, was used to signal to the residents of Marshside that caddies were required at the course. Golf competitions for caddies, arranged by the clubs, were commonplace, and club members sometimes loaned their clubs and even carried them for "their" boy. At Hesketh, after the caddie master had imposed a fine to discipline eighteen boys who had arranged a match amongst themselves without his permission, the boys staged a strike. Their withdrawal of labour was brief and normal service was rapidly restored.[4]

By the early years of the twentieth century, the issue of boy caddies was causing national concern and was raised in Parliament. In 1911, Winston Churchill, the Home Secretary, advocated the use of elderly unemployed men in order to prevent boys entering this "blind alley" occupation. The only practical outcome of the agitation was the formation of a National Caddies' Association: significantly, copies of the pioneering Birkdale scheme were used as a model for this new body. Nevertheless, as late as 1913, almost 4% of all the boys leaving elementary schools in Southport became golf caddies. For Churchtown School, close to the Hesketh Golf Club, the percentage was as high

74. Girl Caddies at Birkdale Golf Club. The eighteenth (now fourth) green.

as 28% of the 25 leavers.[5] It was new National Insurance regulations which required boys to have stamps, which later sounded the death knell to their regular employment as full-time caddies. Schoolboys continued to carry during their holidays and at weekends, whilst each club also developed a cadre of adult caddies. Hesketh Golf Club put on a hot pot supper for as many as 60 caddies in 1935.

Caddying had introduced golf to a wider social audience and, not surprisingly, had created an appetite for playing the game. One way in which working-class men were able to participate in golf was as "artisans". Artisan golfers enjoyed restricted free, or very cheap, golf in return for duties undertaken on the golf course. Many contemporary golf club members think that their attached artisan club is a throw-back to the nineteenth century, when in fact the majority of such clubs are relatively modern twentieth century developments. The Artisan Golfers' Association was formed in 1921 with the object of uniting the various artisan golf clubs in the British Isles into an

75. An Adult Caddie at Hesketh Golf Club. The players are on the eighth green of the old course with Marshside Road in the background.

association and to encourage and help in the formation of new artisan clubs. In fact there were only about half a dozen such clubs in existence at this time. Two of the Association's founding sponsors were J.H. Taylor, the great Open Champion who was a former artisan, and his business partner F.G. Hawtree. It was this pair of course architects who designed Birkdale's new championship layout. Such was the impact of artisan golf, that in 1929, the English Amateur Championship was won by an artisan.

The clubs along the *Line* did not initially follow the precedent established by the Royal Liverpool Club in making provision for local working men to play golf. At Hoylake the local people, particularly the fishermen, resented the presence of the golfers on what they had long, if inaccurately, considered to be common land. They believed that their use of the land for leisure purposes, including watching horse-racing, would be curtailed.[6] They actively opposed golfing – disrupting games, lifting golf balls, and refusing to get off the land. In an attempt to resolve this hiatus the Club gave permission to local residents to play golf on the course. As the Royal Liverpool Club prospered increasing numbers of local men were employed as caddies, and in 1895 the relationship with the local fishing community was formalised into the format of a club – *Hoylake Village Play*. This Club was for local ". . . fishermen, tradesmen and artisans", who had to ". . . be in possession of more than one golf club, one of which had to be wooden headed."[7] The Villagers were allowed to play golf, at restricted times, and in return they were required to help protect the course from vandalism, which was becoming an increasing problem. The Village Play members paid no fees and their numbers grew to over 200. Relationships with the parent Royal Liverpool Club appear to have been cordial: matches between the clubs were played regularly, trophies were donated to the Village Club, and the Villagers produced some outstanding golfers. Although some of its members were professionals, the Village Play Club became affiliated to the Cheshire Golf Union and also joined the Artisan Golfers' Association. Since the Second World War, the explosion in the popularity of golf and the increase in participation has put pressure on golf courses, and clubs have had to review the usage of their courses. At Royal Liverpool it was decided to charge the Village Club members a small fee and the number allowed was progressively reduced. More recently the number of members has been limited to 25 and the subscription waived in lieu of them undertaking formally agreed duties on the course.

West Lancashire was the first club along the *Line* to encourage the participation of working men. The origins of the *West Lancashire Artisans' Golf Club* are unusual and interesting.[8] In 1921 four members of the Crosby Comrades' Club, an ex-servicemen's organisation, wrote to the West Lancashire Club asking if they could play a match on the course. All four were former Club caddies. Following this initiative, the Club offered members of the

76. Royal Liverpool Golf Club – Artisans Spiking the Greens.

Comrades' Club the privilege of playing on the links in return for them undertaking duties on the course. The offer was restricted to members who were former caddies or ex-servicemen. This group became an artisan club in everything but name, but bore the title of the 'Crosby Comrades'. A schism in this club during the 1930s led to the introduction of the name of 'Crosby Villagers'. After World War II, the Club followed the example of the others on the *Line*, and became the West Lancashire Artisan Golf Club. Jack Green was one of the four members of the Comrades' Club who played in the "founding match". Later, playing with only five clubs, he set a course record playing off a handicap of one.

In Formby members of the working class who wanted to play golf, following World War I, adopted the historic pattern established hundreds of years earlier in Scotland. Although the Formby Club links were on the seaward side of the railway, and the Banking and Insurance Club course inland of the railway at Freshfield, there was still abundant 'waste' land close by. These local enthusiasts were able to establish a couple of holes amidst the gorse bushes on the land inland and to the north of Freshfield Station.

This development of a "village club" appeared to be more than a passing fad, and in 1922 it engaged the interest of the Formby Golf Club.⁽⁹⁾ It was decided that the 24 members of the new club could play on the Formby course, with restrictions on time. They had to pay an annual subscription of ten shillings (50p) and undertake certain duties on the course, principally sweeping the greens early on Sunday mornings. A member presented a small hut which served as a pavilion, and the Club, which quickly became known as the *Formby Artisans' Golf Club*, had its own officers and committee to manage its affairs. The Club now enjoys a much improved clubhouse. Although the number of members allowed has been modestly increased over the years, the opportunity to be a member of the Formby Artisans' Club is rightly regarded as a privilege. There have been many family links between the members. A number of players who learnt their golf in this Club went on to become professional golfers.

Improvements in greenkeeping technology, through both equipment and chemicals, has reduced the need for the assistance of artisans on the course. Furthermore, the use of artisan labour became a source of potential conflict with the professional greenkeeping staff. They feared loss of employment, and particularly of overtime. Consequently, artisan duties at Formby have become substantially those of course rangers. Recent years have seen a great increase in the number of people enjoying Formby's sandhills, and the Fisherman's Path across the course is now a much used public right of way. The increase of pedestrian traffic on the course and the ever-present threat of vandalism have placed a premium on ranger duties.

It was September 1931 before the *Birkdale Artisans' Golf Club* was formed.⁽¹⁰⁾ The artisans' principal duties were to sweep the greens on Sunday morning, and to act as rangers. The Artisans' Club was given, and still uses, the old professional's shop, close to the fourth green, as a clubhouse. One of the early members, a gardener, laid out and tended a garden around this clubhouse, thus providing a feast of summer colour. In return for performing their duties, the Birkdale artisans enjoyed free golf, at restricted times. Such is the competition for the limited number of places available in the Club, that it has been suggested that it is far more difficult to become a member of The Royal Birkdale Artisan Club than of the parent Club. Members had to be at least eighteen years old, and, as at Formby, family ties are very strong amongst the artisan membership. One Birkdale artisan, who was estranged from his wife, made and furnished a sophisticated dwelling deep in the dunes of the Birkdale course. The stove of his underground home could only be lit at night so that tell-tale smoke would not reveal the den's secret location.

Philip Irlam, the historian of the *Hillside Club*, has uncovered the existence of an Hillside artisan section during the 1930s.⁽¹¹⁾ It appears that artisans undertook ranging duties, as in 1936 the Club purchased badges for them. There is also an entry in the suggestion book that artisans should act as fore-caddies for the

77. Birkdale Artisan Golf Club 1935. This group, displaying the Club's trophies, is photographed in front of their clubhouse, formerly the professional's shop.

blind drive, over a hill, at the sixteenth. The Hillside artisan section did not survive the Second World War. *Southport and Ainsdale Golf Club*, Hillside's close neighbour across the *Line*, appears to have had an artisan section since 1937.

Hesketh Golf Club's artisans only came into being as late as 1938.[12] Originally formed with only twelve members, the artisan section was managed by a sub-committee of the Green Committee. The artisans were allowed cheap golf in return for duties. Initially they met in the greenkeeper's hut, a venue which reflected their perceived status. They later met in a shed in the garden of one of the course-side cottages. Following the Second World War a shed was erected on club land, and the number of members increased. The artisans were local men, and as at the other artisan clubs the members achieved a high standard of play. The maximum handicap for membership was as low as fourteen. The Artisan Club flourished and was reconstituted in 1955, with decreased numbers. The shell of an old property, close to the seventeenth tee, has been made into an attractive clubhouse, and the Club presently has 30 members. An artisan golfer's annual subscription of £4 to the parent golf club was waived in 1971.

The artisan clubs are run with similar conventions to those of the parent clubs. They have their own officers, including a Captain. Members of all the artisan clubs along the *Line* are able to enjoy a programme of competitions on their home courses, whilst inter-club matches are played with members of other artisan clubs. In 1958 a past Captain of the defunct Freshfield Golf Club presented the Allan Cup for competition between the artisan clubs along the *Line* – West Lancashire, Formby, Southport and Ainsdale, Royal Birkdale and Hesketh. Clubhouse Honours Boards and annual prize giving evenings are features of the artisan clubs.

Ranging and the filling and seeding of divot holes appear to be the major duties for contemporary artisans. The former can be an unpleasant, even dangerous, task when faced by truculent trespassers. Divotting, also, is not without danger. Tragically, one artisan lost an eye after being hit by a golf ball whilst divotting on the Hesketh course. More recently, the Hesketh artisan members have been encouraged to employ their trade skills to make course improvements, such as fences and bridges.

In the 1930s, as the number of artisan clubs increased, the Artisan Golfers' Association was anticipating something like 200,000 working-class men being enabled to play golf ". . . according to its highest traditions."[13] The concept of artisan golf now sits uneasily in Prime Minister Major's vision of a classless society. The social identification of artisan golfers can no longer be made with the certainty and clarity of the 1930s. Some club members, facing ever increasing fees, wonder if the concept of the artisan golfer is now a social anachronism. Several local clubs have admitted former members of artisan clubs as full members, although none has yet followed the example of the Wentworth Club in abolishing the artisan section whilst offering former artisans the opportunity to become full members. A long-standing member of one of the artisan clubs along the *Line* recently won almost a quarter of a million pounds in a competition. He chose to continue to play his golf as an artisan, with his old friends. His position highlights the current difficulty with the concept of "artisan golfer". What is the contemporary rationale for artisan golf, and what are the criteria for being an artisan as we approach the millennium?

Municipally sponsored golf is another source of budget golf. In Scotland local councils have long acted as providers of golf. Some of the most famous links, such as St. Andrews, are public. This provision was cited by one of the early advocates of a public course in Southport:

"Evidence could be secured by a visit to St. Andrews on a summer evening, when the hardy sons of toil, released from their strenuous lives, seek recuperation on the links on the coast side, where the land is town property."[14]

Contemporary photographs show local fishermen sharing a few clubs as they play on the already famous Old Course. Perhaps a better example of a municipal golf course catering for large numbers of working-class golfers was that on the Braid Hills in Edinburgh at 2d (less than 1p) a round.

Early in the twentieth century, several English authorities provided municipal golf courses. The superior south coast residential town of Bournemouth was one of the earliest, but the green fee of a shilling (5p) suggests that this was not for the working man. F.G. Hawtree, one of the pioneers of the Artisan Golfers' Association, also devised the idea of a National Association of Public Golf Courses, and his partner J.H. Taylor presented a challenge shield for players on such courses.

Agitation for a municipal course in Southport first appeared in the form of letters to local newspapers in 1905. One correspondent suggested the use of spare land behind the gasworks on the inland margin of the town at Blowick. He argued that the corporation would gain both fees from the golfers and fares for the trams. This land was indeed used for a golf course but it was provided not by the authority, but by a local doctor – W.A. Findlay. He founded the Southport Athletic Golf Club. (The Southport Athletic Club had its grounds at Blowick.) The fees for the new golf club were five shillings a year (25p), which would put it within the pocket of skilled tradesmen and small shopkeepers. As we have seen, in 1907 Findlay rented the former Grosvenor Golf Club course in Birkdale and founded the Blundell Club, whose membership fees, although modest, were over four times those of the Athletic Golf Club. Findlay's energy and initiative appeared to have no bounds: he was also responsible for founding a local miniature rifle club.

Findlay was elected to the Southport Council and he became the champion of the campaign for a municipal golf course. Having trained in Edinburgh, Findlay would have been familiar with that city's Braid Hills' Municipal Course. He repeatedly raised the issue in the Council arguing that a municipal course in Southport would not only provide an amenity for residents and visitors, but would also generate income. He met a blanket of obfuscation. Opponents pointed to the six existing courses in Southport and Birkdale. Findlay consistently re-affirmed that what he wanted was a municipal golf course, which would provide golf for "the masses". He claimed that, unlike football, golf was a game for players not spectators:

"Whenever working men had an opportunity to play golf at a reasonable price they not only entered into it but enjoyed it and benefited by it."[15]

By 1911 his persistence appears to have convinced his fellow Councillors: these included one opponent of the scheme who was a former Captain of one of the local golf clubs. Prevarication on location followed, but 50 acres of reclaimed foreshore at the northern end of the Promenade were finally selected. The Council spent £1500 for the laying of a nine-hole course, of some 2900 yards in length, and

78. Southport Municipal Golf Links – aerial view 1930s. This photograph shows the course on reclaimed beach land. Part of the beach can be seen in the foreground.

for the building of a pavilion. Some of the money was spent on strengthening the embankment in order to resist high tides. Advice on the layout of the course was taken from Peter McEwan, the professional at the nearby Hesketh links. Draining the low-lying land posed problems that have still not been fully answered. The pavilion, a wooden building painted in green and white stripes, was situated off Park Road. The accommodation included locker rooms and clubrooms for gentlemen and ladies, and there was a verandah overlooking the course.

The new course was opened in 1912. In fixing the fees – £1-1s (£1.05) per year for both men and women, with charges of 6d for nine holes and 9d for eighteen holes – the Council ". . . endeavoured to ensure that they shall not under-cut some of the struggling golf clubs in the district." The Chairman of the responsible committee believed that the opening of a municipal course

". . . would prove not to be a disadvantage to the existing golf clubs, but a feeder to these clubs. People would come to these links and obtain a certain level of proficiency when they would want to get amongst the experts."[16]

The YMCA Club, playing out-of-town on the old Southport Club links at Blowick, would have been particularly vulnerable to this new competition. Its golf fees were the same as those of the municipal course, although members had also to pay an additional general fee of half a guinea (52p) to the YMCA. In commenting on the opening of the municipal links, the Secretary of the YMCA thought that it would be a course for beginners and would not adversely affect the YMCA. As at the YMCA, the Council decided against Sunday play on the new links. A local sports' outfitter seized the opportunity afforded by the opening of the Municipal Links to advertise a beginners' golf set – four clubs (driver, iron, mashie and putter), a bag, and one rubber-cored ball – all for the bargain price of a guinea (£1.05).

A spokesman for the Town Council suggested that if the municipal course was successful then the present links would be reserved exclusively for women, and another eighteen-hole course for men established. In the event this did not happen, although the course was well patronised and extended to eighteen holes in 1932, and a 'Par Three' course was opened on the sea-front Prince's Park in 1933. The Municipal Links has provided a home for a number of local clubs and societies, the principal one being *The Park Club* which has a well appointed clubhouse alongside the thirties'-style pavilion and café, which replaced the old wooden structure. Many Southport club golfers still start their golf careers on this course before moving on.

79. Southport Municipal Golf Links – Pavilion. The 1930s style architecture is reminiscent of Royal Birkdale.

116

80. Southport Municipal Golf Links – Park Club Clubhouse.

REFERENCES

(1)   *Birkdale Board School Log Book* 8th February 1899.
(2)   Johnson, A.J.D. *The Royal Birkdale Golf Club 1889–1989* (1989), p.22.
(3)   Marsden, W.E. *The Development of the Educational Facilities of Southport 1825–1944* (1959) M.A. Thesis, Sheffield University.
(4)   Dixon, N. *Hesketh Ladies* (1989), p.11.
(5)   *Southport Education Committee Year Book 1913–1914* (1914), pp.126–128.
(6)   Spence, J. *The Story of the Royal Liverpool Village Play 1895–1995* (1995), p.4.
(7)   *Ibid.*, p.6.
(8)   Edwards, L. *The West Lancashire Golf Club* (1973), p.13.
(9)   Thomas, I.S. *Formby Golf Club 1884–1972* (1972), p.154.
(10) Anon. *Birkdale Golf Club Golden Jubilee 1889–1939* (1939), p.2.
(11) Irlam, P. *A Lively Octogenarian: Hillside Golf Club 1911–1991* (1993), p.51.
(12) Lawless, P. (Ed.) *The Golfer's Companion* (1938), p.400.
(13) Hick, K. *The Hesketh Golf Club 1885–1985* (1985), p.222.
(14) *S.V.* 27th July 1907.
(15) *S.V.* 26th August 1909.
(16) *S.V.* 7th July 1912.

CHAPTER NINE

REFLECTIONS FROM THE 'NINETEENTH HOLE'

Harold Hilton the great local Open Champion introduced a Lancashire and Yorkshire Railway Company booklet, *Where to Golf*, with the statement that:

> "There is no game in the world which is quite so dependent upon the facilities in connection with Railway travelling as the Royal and Ancient Game of Golf. In order to find ground which is in any way suitable for the best links, it is necessary to explore tracts of country far away from the City, in lonely areas of the kingdom where the land has escaped the hand of the agriculturalist."[1]

He went on to describe the role of the railway companies in promoting the game:

> "It must be acknowledged that the courtesy and far seeing policy of our railway companies have done very much to popularise the game. They have willingly done their utmost in many ways to meet the requirements of Golfers, not only by running special trains to well-known Golfing centres, and stopping others which otherwise would have passed through the stations contiguous to the links, but in many cases having erected special stations as near as possible to certain courses."

These congratulatory statements were, of course, commissioned for the railway company publicity material. Nevertheless Hilton does acknowledge that the railway companies made concessions, including ". . . the privilege of golfer's tickets", not out of philanthropy but in order to generate profit. The close relationship between the railway companies and golf clubs, however, was normally beneficial to both. The *Line*, run by The Liverpool, Crosby and Southport Railway Company (and later The Lancashire and Yorkshire Railway Company), was fundamental to the development of the high-class residential commuter settlements on the coastal strip to the north of Liverpool, and played a major role in the emergence of its golf courses.

In this age of the motor car the proximity of Hall Road Station is no longer relevant to the West Lancashire Golf Club. The fact that the original clubhouse adjoined the station was, however, a critical factor in the early years of the Club. The railway was not only vital to the residential development of Blundellsands, it also made the golf course very accessible from the city. Similarly the railway was important not only to the residential development of Freshfield, but also to Formby Golf Club. It was only the railway's ability to bring golfers directly to the course, that enabled Formby to progress from being a small neighbourhood club to becoming one of Lancashire's major golfing venues. The controversy over the playing of golf on Sundays at the West Lancashire and Formby clubs, and the provision of dormy accommodation at the latter reflect the role of the railway in bringing golfers to these courses.

Unlike West Lancashire and Formby, Birkdale was principally a neighbourhood club serving residents of Birkdale Park, a very successful high-class residential suburb. In addition, the Birkdale course and clubhouse were well removed from the railway station and consequently the *Line* was of less direct significance in the Birkdale Golf Club's development, although it had been crucial to that of the Birkdale suburb.

The *Line* played relatively little part in the story of the Southport/Hesketh Club. In fact it was mainly the railway line from Manchester that brought golfers from inland Lancashire to Southport. Nevertheless, the *Line* was important in enabling Southport members to play their part in the community of golfers along the coast.

The second generation of golf clubs along the *Line* – Southport and Ainsdale, Blundell, Liverpool Banking and Insurance, and later Hillside – were geographically quite close together and surrounded by relatively undeveloped land. Consequently, there was not a sufficient pool of potential members living in the immediate neighbourhood to adequately support all four clubs, and the railway, with its newly installed electric service, was crucial to their development, permitting easy access for golfers from the Liverpool district.

The golf clubs along the *Line* were on the property of three separate landowners. Although the relationships between the three estates and the golf clubs differed, all three recognised and profited from the beneficial effects the presence of golf clubs had on high-class residential development.

Although the landowner, Nicholas Blundell, did not originally promote The West Lancashire Golf Club, he was instrumental in attracting it to Blundellsands. From the beginning the fortunes of the Club were closely related to his residential suburb, which it helped to develop. The advance of the Blundellsands villas always posed a threat to the West Lancashire Club, with the Estate wanting to repossess land from the course for more profitable housing. In the event the Club was able to capitalise on its successive re-locations and improve the quality of the links. West Lancashire is now the only golf club along the *Line* where the land is still owned by the original estate, and where a harmonious link with the landowner, acting as Club President, has been maintained.

The landowner, Charles Weld-Blundell, played no part in the beginnings of Formby Golf Club when the founders rented land from one of his tenant farmers. As the Club prospered Weld-Blundell did lease land directly to the Club and it was at this point that he briefly assumed the Presidency. That he did not continue in this office was consistent with the idiosyncratic, and rather mercurial, nature of the man. He maintained no long lasting associations with institutions in the north west. Not a golfer, he was very much an absentee landowner spending much of his time at his homes in London and at Lulworth Castle, where he could indulge his passions respectively for the literary life and for sailing. Continental holidays also figured prominently in the family calendar. Visits to Ince Blundell Hall were infrequent and often brief. Formby Golf Club represented a pawn in his larger chess game of suburban development. He recognised the importance of golf as an attraction for a residential estate. Nevertheless, like the Blundell family in their dealings with the West Lancashire Club, he was willing to repossess parts of the golf course when the Freshfield villa builders wanted the land. As at Formby, it was local enthusiasts who brought the Birkdale Golf Club into being. Charles Weld-Blundell, ever the commercial opportunist, was prepared to take advantage of this venture, but even though he was the Club President he did little to help the Club. His policy of granting it only short leases would have allowed him to require it to move from part, or indeed all of its course, if the demand for building land had been sufficient to justify moving the links.

By the early twentieth century Charles Weld-Blundell was well persuaded of the beneficial effects of golf course development on his dune lands. At best it stimulated housing, at worst there was a steady income from what was very marginal agricultural land, which the golf club would improve with drains and fertilisers. Most of the day-to-day dealings with the clubs were handled by his agent, but the strategy would be the landowner's. In the re-location of the Blundell, Southport and Ainsdale and Hillside Clubs the Estate was reacting to their initiatives. In the case of the Banking and Insurance Club, such was Weld-Blundell's anxiety to realise his ambitions for Ainsdale-on-Sea, the Estate assumed an unusually pro-active posture.

The migrations of the Southport/Hesketh Club reflect the rivalry between the two local landowners and their wish to have the golf course, with the associated benefits to villa development, on their land. Uniquely for a club along the *Line*, the landowner, Edward Fleetwood Hesketh was an active founder member. It was only later, after his death, that the golf club became part of the residential jig-saw. Charles Scarisbrick, the owner of the Moss Lane course, was also an active founder member of the Club. Anxious to re-vitalise villa development in Hesketh Park, Charles Hesketh Bibby Hesketh brought a new concept to the relationship between land owners and golf clubs along the *Line*. As proprietor, he acted positively laying out the course and building the clubhouse, the Club was to learn that there was a price to pay for such apparent "generosity". Surviving brochures show that the landed estates all used the proximity of golf courses as a major inducement in their attempts to attract tenants for their development schemes.[2]

A very significant factor in the development of the early clubs along the *Line*, was the emergence of a local golfing community many of whom were members at more than one of the clubs. Members of the Royal Liverpool Club were influential in the founding of the West Lancashire Club, and similar bonds can be seen in the foundation of the Formby, Southport and Birkdale clubs. Being a member of more than one of these relatively closely-clustered kindred clubs continued to be a feature of the area. At the annual dinners of most of the golf clubs along the *Line*, the Captains of The Royal Liverpool Golf Club and The West Lancashire Golf Club are involved in the toasts. Although changed economic circumstances now preclude extensive plurality of membership, many strong sporting and social bonds between the clubs are still evident. Since 1908, there has been a very active Society of Liverpool Golf Captains; whilst inter-club competitions at all levels are a feature of golf along the *Line*.

A relatively new but crucially important player in the story of golf along the *Line* is the local authority. It was the intervention of the Southport County Borough Council that enabled the Birkdale, Hesketh and Hillside golf clubs to preserve their courses when the Weld-Blundell and Hesketh Estates were wanting to sell these assets off and there was a real danger of some of the land being used for building development. The Southport and Ainsdale Club lost potential development land in the southwards re-location of its course but the Weld-Blundell Estate retained ownership until the golf club bought the freehold in 1964. In buying the Birkdale, Hesketh and Hillside courses and leasing them to the clubs, the Council recognised their importance as tourist attractions and as amenities in residential areas. The local authority's foresight has been well rewarded. During the 1930s Hesketh, Birkdale, Southport and Ainsdale, and Hillside were all to act as hosts for the Dunlop Southport Professional Tournament, whilst Southport and Ainsdale hosted the prestigious Ryder Cup competition against the Americans during this period. The local authority had insisted that the Birkdale course be developed to championship standard and a new clubhouse be built, targets which the Club quickly achieved. Major competitions were successfully hosted and the Club, which now regularly stages 'The Open', was granted the coveted 'Royal' designation in 1951, a fitting tribute to the Club's remarkable achievements.

In the cases of the Hesketh and Hillside clubs the local authority did exchange some land from the existing courses for land of lesser commercial value. At Hesketh, the loss of some sand-hill holes for low-lying re-claimed estuary land probably diminished the quality of the course, whilst the move deeper into the sand-hills at Hillside allowed the Club to create one of the finest back nine holes in these islands. Nevertheless the local authority continued to be a municipal fairy godmother to the golf clubs, particularly in respect of extending the leases to 999 years. A by-product of the 1975 local government re-organisation is that all the golf courses along the *Line* are now part of the Metropolitan Borough of Sefton, thus allowing it to advertise itself as "The Golfing Centre of Europe".

Society in late nineteenth century England was stratified on social class lines and institutions reflected what were often subtle divisions. In the early years of the development of golf along the *Line* the clubs had a rather uniform upper middle-class base, reflected in the number of individuals who were members of more than one of the clubs. It is interesting to note that by 1910, the fees at the Hesketh and Birkdale clubs were the same, although they were lower than those of the West Lancashire and Formby clubs, which were also the same. In and around Southport there were a number of clubs competing for members and with the formation of further new clubs – Southport and Ainsdale, Blundell, Freshfield and Hillside – a clear hierarchy emerged, in terms of the fees charged. Provision at the lower rungs of this hierarchy was provided by the Y.M.C.A. and the local authority, through its municipal golf course. During the thirties, the game's social base was further widened with the introduction, by the major local clubs, of artisan sections.

Golf Clubs along the 'Line': Fees c.1910

	Entrance	Annual	Green
Gentlemen			
West Lancashire	£15.75	£4.20	£0.12
Formby	£15.75	£4.20	£0.12
Hesketh	£10.50	£2.62	£0.12
Birkdale	£10.50	£2.62	£0.12
Banking & Insurance	£ 5.25	£3.15	£0.12
Southport & Ainsdale	£ 5.25	£2.10	£0.10
Blundell (Birkdale)	£ 1.05	£1.05	£0.05
Y.M.C.A.		£1.57	
Southport Municipal		£1.02	£0.03
Ladies			
Formby	£ 5.25	£2.10	£0.05
West Lancashire	£ 5.25	£2.10	£0.12

Source: *Lancashire and Yorkshire Railway: Where to Golf.*

The golf clubs in this area provide an illustration of a variety of different ways in which pioneer lady golfers participated in this male-dominated game in the late nineteenth century. Their position mirrored the relationships between the sexes which was evident in other aspects of contemporary society. Not surprisingly we find that ladies were frequently restricted to the status of 'associate' members, paying reduced subscriptions and being subject to playing restrictions. Where ladies' clubs and committees existed their functions were largely limited to the organisation of competitions and the supervision of handicaps. Nevertheless from the earliest years women had been welcomed into the clubs and were actively participating in the game. Indeed, the area was exceptional in having two ladies' clubs with their own courses and clubhouses. The situation of the West Lancashire Ladies' Club, which the ladies ran, was particularly noteworthy.

The golf clubs along the *Line* have inherited an extraordinarily rich golfing heritage. Evolution and changing economic circumstances have altered the area's social fabric and there are corresponding changes within the clubs. Nevertheless, the clubs continue to improve their courses and clubhouses, whilst their traditions, so firmly established by earlier generations, continue to provide the yardstick against which their affairs are conducted. Along the south-west Lancashire coast, the community of golfers has taken advantage of what Bernard Darwin described as ". . . a noble stretch of golfing ground which is second to none", in order to produce a magical cluster of golf courses. The largely forgotten roles played by the landowners, the railway, and the local authority were critical to this development.

REFERENCES

(1) Hilton, H. "Where to Golf" *ABC Guide to the Towns and Pleasure Resorts upon the Lancashire and Yorkshire Railway* (c.1910) p.212.
(2) See for example: Weld-Blundell Estate *Seaside Garden Village: Ainsdale* (1908) and Southport Corporation *Make Your Home in Sunny Southport* (1927) including details of Southport Corporation , Weld-Blundell and Hesketh housing developments.